DANNY SARROS

Mel

First published by COLD FRONT PUBLISHING 2021

Copyright © 2021 by Danny Sarros

All rights reserved. No part of this publication may be reproduced, stored or transmitted in any form or by any means, electronic, mechanical, photocopying, recording, scanning, or otherwise without written permission from the publisher. It is illegal to copy this book, post it to a website, or distribute it by any other means without permission.

This novel is entirely a work of fiction. The names, characters and incidents portrayed in it are the work of the author's imagination. Any resemblance to actual persons, living or dead, events or localities is entirely coincidental.

Danny Sarros asserts the moral right to be identified as the author of this work.

Danny Sarros has no responsibility for the persistence or accuracy of URLs for external or third-party Internet Websites referred to in this publication and does not guarantee that any content on such Websites is, or will remain, accurate or appropriate.

Designations used by companies to distinguish their products are often claimed as trademarks. All brand names and product names used in this book and on its cover are trade names, service marks, trademarks and registered trademarks of their respective owners. The publishers and the book are not associated with any product or vendor mentioned in this book. None of the companies referenced within the book have endorsed the book.

Danny Sarros is solely responsible for the content of this novel.

Second edition

ISBN: 978-1-7379662-3-4

This book was professionally typeset on Reedsy.
Find out more at reedsy.com

To the three greatest women in my life, my grandmother, my mother and my wife. Eula Mae Gilbert, Mildred L. Sarros & Christine E. Sarros.

Foreword

واورلجال العظام المشي بينكم، ولكن سيتم ملء
عينيك
 وسوف نقدم لكل مساعدة من العقل أو
مع غبار الحياة.
من
ان حية.
الرجال مثل هذه، للحافظ عليه ويشرفني، ألأنها
ليست
سوى عدد قليل.

Translation of Ancient Arabic Text

"Great men will walk among you, yet your eyes will be filled with the dust of life. They will offer you the help of mind or hand. Men, such as these are to be cherished and honored, for they are but few.

Author Unknown 923 B.C.

"This Melchizedek was a king of the city of Salem, and also a priest of the Most High God. When Abraham was returning home after winning a great battle against many kings, Melchizedek met him and blessed him; then Abraham took a tenth of all he had won in battle and gave it to Melchizedek. Melchizedek's name means "Justice," so he is the King of Justice; and he is also the King of Peace because of the name of his city, Salem, which means "Peace." Melchizedek had no father or mother and there is no record of any of his ancestors. He was never born and he never died but his life is like that of the Son of God...a priest forever."

Hebrews 7:1-3 The Living Bible

Chapter 1

He sat thumbing through the remains of what once was the morning paper. The sterile odor of antiseptic lay heavy in the air. A constant bustle in the hallway and foreign names over the intercom made thumbing easy and reading difficult. Lying in the bed next to his chair was the small-framed body of a ninety-four-year-old woman. Her once long flowing hair was cropped short, making it easier to care for. The light brown and blonde tones had long been replaced by soft white coloring accented by dashes of gray. Her aged, spotted skin slipped over her frail bones like an afghan over the arm of a rocking chair.

Breathing was the only labor she could perform at the end of life's day. As she lay there, he was oblivious to her condition, her age, their surroundings. In his mind, she was the definition of strength, determination, and goodness. From boyhood, he remembered waking every morning to find this woman sitting in her housecoat, eating breakfast as she fed her soul on the Word of God. Countless times he would find his little legs going from a mad dash to tippytoes through her kitchen as Grandma sat silently in conversation with her Lord, "payin' no never mind" to the noises children make that most adults find distracting.

Grandma was a product of the old Deep South. A time when poor meant little or nothing, yet he never recalled her complaining about her youth. Her gratitude to a great and mighty God for walking with her through it all was well known. She was quick to identify those blessings she had been given. She knew the wealth of a loving God and had experienced it completely. She had accepted His grace as a child, and now that relationship which sustained her through life was what she was ready to embrace in death.

He folded the paper and placed it on the cold tile next to the chair. He rose quietly to bring the covers up to her neck as she had done for him a thousand bedtimes ago. Her eyes opened slowly; they were slightly bloodshot and watery.

"Hey, boy," she smiled in recognition.

"Hey, Grammy. Can I get you something?"

"Oh, just a few ice chips would be nice," she requested sweetly.

"Sure, sure."

He hastily scooped the chips from the water

pitcher on the nearby table. Gently he placed a teaspoonful to her dry, drawn lips. She took them with a familiar smile of gratefulness. Her eyes beamed brightly, proud of the boy before her. He loved her and she, him. She weakly patted the edge of the bed.

"Sit here. There are things I must tell you."

"Grammy," he started, "you just rest; we can talk later."

"Hush," she softly commanded. "If'n I want to talk, I'll talk."

He smiled and didn't dare press the issue. Gingerly he distributed his weight on the bed so as not to disturb his grandmother's comfort.

"I want to tell you 'bout a man I met when I was a little girl," she began.

He lovingly brushed the uncombed hair back from her forehead.

"Now, you pay attention, boy. This old woman still has a few more stories left to tell. It was the spring of 1915. The magnolias were in bloom an' the children were tastin' the sweet nectar of the honeysuckle blossom. I was eleven years old. Life on the farm was hard. I had no idea'r how hard it was; it was all I knew. It was a warm day, a Friday after school. Back behind our house an' barn was that stand of woods. There was this small ravine with a piddle of a creek runnin' through it. Even on the hottest days, the shade of those trees an' the coolness of that old creek gave me an' brother Bill a wonderful place ta explore an' play. Little Bill loved ta hunt those woods fer rabbits an' squirrels. He always walked back there with his rifle. Member, the one I gave you? That little .22 single shot."

"Yeah, Grammy, I still have it," he assured.

The old woman continued. "Oh, little Bill was runnin' up at the top of the ravine. Holdin' that gun by the barrel, I was splash'n in the creek throwin' sticks in, watchin' the current carry 'em downstream. I happened ta look up an' saw little Bill swing'in' 'round in a circle, holdin' his gun by the barrel. Now, this was somethin' Papa had warned him 'bout when he first went an' give him the gun. 'Safety,' Papa said, 'Safety first.'

"Well, everythin' kinda slowed down. I 'member little Bill slipped on some loose dirt, an' as he started ta fall he tried ta catch himself by stick'n the butt of that gun out into the ground. There was this loud crack that echoed up an' down the ravine, a sound not uncommon ta an afternoon in the woods. After the gun fired, a silence fell on our special place. I watched as little Bill rolled down the hill like a sack o' potatoes. He was all limp an' quiet. He ended up in the creek. The water was runnin' all over an' 'round him. As I got closer, I pushed my long curls back out of my eyes."

"I saw dark, red blood mixin' with the water an' little Bill's shirt was wet with both. He just lay there; I couldn't even call his name. He didn't move. His little chest didn't rise up an' down like it did at night when he was sleepin' on his feather bed. His eyes were open, but they didn't blink. They were kinda like a catfish that's been laid up on the bank fer a while. No matter how hard I tried, words just wouldn't come."

The boy looked intently at his grandmother. He had never heard this story before. He was mesmerized by its clarity, detail, and unfamiliarity.

"That's when I first saw him," she said quietly.

"Saw who, Grammy?" he asked.

"Mel. He came from behind an' walked right past me."

"Looks like this young'un took a spill."

"He looked back at me with a smile as he knelt beside Bill. He was bent over my little brother an' I was still unable ta speak. The stranger picked little Bill up. At first, I thought he was crazy! Couldn't he see my brother was dead, or soon ta be? Then all of a sudden little Bill began ta sputter an' wipe the water from his face."

"Ohhhh, my side," he yelled.

"I stepped closer in, prayin' what I was seein' was true! Little Bill lifted his shirt an' there was a red welt where the rifle barrel had poked him.

"That'll be sore a few days, son," the stranger observed. "You just

might learn a lesson 'bout treatin' firearms with more respect."

"Little Bill just looked at the stranger, wide-eyed an' glad he wasn't Pa, cause Pa would've switched him good! My fears an' shock quickly turned ta motherly anger, an' the words began ta flow. You git yourself up that hill an' git that gun, Billy Ray. NOW! I was really hollerin," Grammy chuckled, "him puttin' me through all that fright. I watched my baby brother climb that hill holdin' his side."

"That was some pretty dangerous foolin' 'round by that boy," the stranger said in a soft voice.

"I thought he was bleedin' there in the water," her voice trailed off in wonder.

"People see an' don't see thin's every day, Pumpkin, but the closer your stand'in' to the truth, the clearer things are. How 'bout I walk you an' your brother over to your house?"

"I felt safe an' comfortable with this man. I was glad he had come along when he did. Now, all I wanted ta do is tell Pa what happened."

"Don't you be tattlin' on me, Eula Mae!" little Bill yelled as he was makin' his way to his gun.

Billy stopped at the top of the rise. I saw him bendin' over to pick up his rifle. "Oh, Pa's gonna blister me!" he screamed. "My gun's busted!"

He was right. We didn't have much, but what we had was in good condition an' oughtta be kept that way. 'If'n ya take care of your stock, it'll last ferever.' That's what Pa always said. I thought ferever was a pretty long time, but I knew what he was sayin. Little Bill stood there; he looked like he'd been through the mill."

"You busted it good," Mel commented as he looked over the object of Billy's demise. "I know a bit 'bout. Fixin' wood, I think I can take care of this if your pa wants me to."

"With that hope, we slowly walked back to the farmhouse. You 'member our house, don't ya boy?"

"Yes, Grammy. We were there for a family reunion when I was fifteen.

"Yes, that's right," she affirmed. "Two-story, white house with four bitty bedrooms upstairs, a creaky wooden kitchen floor an' six big old Cottonwoods guardin' the outside. Those trees must've been 150 years old." Grammy thought back, soakin' up the sights and sounds of her youth.

"When we got near the house," Grammy continued, "Pa was standin' with his back ta us, fillin' the pig trough with feed. Now your great gran'pa didn't cotton ta strangers. If you were kin, or a friend he'd do anythin' fer you. If he didn't know you . . . well, he wasn't blessed with the gift of hospitality. When we got close enough ta where Pa could hear us over the squealin' pigs, he turned, expectin' ta see little Bill an' me. Pa didn't even look at Billy or me."

"Can I help you, mister?" Pa asked.

"No, sir, I was just walkin' these two home. I come upon 'em in the woods over there. The boy had taken a fall an' busted his gun." The stranger gave Pa a relaxed smile an' scratched his head."

"I probably wouldn't have noticed 'em if I hadn't heard the shot. I thought someone was shootin' at me fer a minute, 'til I 'membered no one knows me in these parts," Mel continued his grin.

Pa returned a faint acknowledgment of the joke an' turned his attention towards little Bill. "Boy, was you foolin' 'round out there with that gun?"

"Pa, I slipped on some rocks. I . . . I was chasin' down a big old rabbit. The next thin' I know this man was helpin' me up. Honest!"

"Little Bill looked at me, not sure how much I had seen. I wanted ta tell Pa how Billy almost killed himself, but fer some reason, I held my tongue."

'Go wash up. First, hand me that rifle.' "Pa finally saw up close how

bad it had been broken."

"I can repair that stock. I happen to have been a cabinet-maker a while back. I'm sure you could do a fine job, but it wouldn't be no bother fer me to do it. By the way, my name's Mel." Mel extended his hand in friendship.

Pa took his hand. "I'm Otis, Otis Gilbert."

"Mel stood there tall an' lanky, a bit of a raggedy man, Momma would say. His clothes were clean but well worn, a bit shiny. Mel had a satchel over his shoulder. I guessed it was his house, a place he kept all his worldly possessions. He was a little younger than Pa. His spirit an' skin was a lot softer. The thing I never fergot 'bout Mel were his eyes. They were honest, carin' an' happy. His left eye was half brown an' half green, right down the middle, never saw anythin' like it. I tried not ta stare, but that's hard fer a young'un. Still, over the next few weeks ta come, I would steal glances from time ta time. Pa an' Mel were just standin' there talkin' a bit when Pa said, "Mel, there's a work shed over there just behind the barn. You'll find what you need ta fix the boy's gun. Go 'head an' see what'cha can do."

Mel smiled. "Thanks, that would give me some pleasure."

"Eula!" called Pa. "Go git me an' Mel a glass of sweet tea.'

"Yes sir, Pa." An' I was off ta the kitchen. Momma had been watchin' from the window. The screen door cracked behind me."

"Who's that man out there with your pa?"

"I think she was surprised Pa just didn't send Mel off on his way.

"His name is Mel. We met him in the woods; Little

Bill fell down an' busted up his gun. He could've kilt himself!" I added as prissy as I could, "Mel picked him up, brushed him off, an' walked us home. Pa asked fer some tea fer him an' Mel. Mel's gonna fix little Bill's gun."

"Mr. Mel, Darlin'. Address him as Mr. Mel," Momma corrected.

"Momma seemed a bit perplexed; I didn't know if it was Pa's behavior or all the information I bubbled out. But when Pa wanted his tea, he wanted it now. I walked, careful not ta spill a drop. The glasses were startin' ta sweat before I reached Pa. Here you go!" I said as I handed him an excuse ta sit down fer a minute. I looked 'round an' Mel was gone."

"Go 'head an' take that tea ta Mr. Mel in the shed, an' don't be gittin' in his way."

"As I got outta sight 'round the barn, just before I reached the shed, I took a sip of tea. I'd always sneak a sip when I could. If I got caught, I'd catch it good! Cause it's impolite, but someone else's tea always tasted sweeter."

"When I got ta the shed, Mel was standin' at Pa's workbench. Mel had already taken the barrel off the gun. Mel was studyin' the cracked stock."

"How's that tea?" Mel asked me.

"There was no window Mel could have looked out. I'm sure it's cold an' sweet, just the way Momma always makes it," I assured him. "Mel smiled as he took the glass. He held it up ta the light. I was thinkin' he was lookin' fer my lip prints on the rim."

"A touch of lemon, too," he added with a smile of someone who knew the secrets of the universe, an' certain little girls.

"Generally speakin', most adults I had known were always busy bein' adults. They had a hard time enjoyin' an afternoon or watchin' hummin'birds sip juice from a flower. They were busy with their responsibilities an' makin' out their importance ta everyone 'round. I didn't sense Mel had ta puff himself up one bit. He was special. I could tell. Maybe kids sense things like that, things adults miss. We both knew I had sipped his tea, but he didn't care. He took a few swallows an' placed the glass towards the back of the bench, as not ta spill it. Then he pulled back the flap on his satchel an' retrieved a wooden box. It was a beautiful box all engraved, with a fancy brass latch. I couldn't wait ta see what it held inside. Mel could see my anticipation an' lifted me up on the bench fer a closer look."

"This box contains some gifts God gave me."

"Before he opened it, he sipped his tea. That's when I got a good look at the box. It was all dovetailed corners, 'bout the size of a shoebox. On the lid, an' sides were all kinds of carvin's. There was a big boat with all kinds of animals gittin' on fer a ride. There were people walkin' through the middle of a lake. There was a star an' a cross an' a lot of symbols an' words I didn't recognize. I knew there was some powerful religious stuff inside. Why he brought it out, I had no idea'r. He unlocked that fancy scrolled brass latch an' pushed open the lid. Inside I was surprised ta see small bottles, an' there must've been two-dozen little engravin' tools. There were files of every size, an' some chisels."

"Each of these tools has a special purpose," Mel explained ta me. "If you notice the end of this graver; its shape is a small 'v.' Now, with this tool, I can engrave very fine detail, like feathers on a bird or leaves on a tree. Now you see, this graver has a kinda scoop-tipped blade. I can use that one to help a carvin' stan' out. It's called 'carved in relief.'"

"You have a lot of 'em graver things."

"Yes, Pumpkin, I do. You see, all of these tools are different. They have one purpose an' in the hand of a master craftsman they can produce beautiful an' intricate scenes an' designs. But cha gotta 'member one tool can't do everythin' - each has a special purpose."

"I just sat an' listened.

"Do you go to church?" Mel asked me.

"Most times sir – not Pa so much. Pa says there's lots of men who go there an' durin' the week they'll cheat a man out of a day's wages if'n he can. Others come in an' sin' the songs an' ya still can smell the whiskey on their breath from the night before!" I explained this ta Mel in a gentle an' plain ways, so as not ta upset him.

"You see, my Pa won't have any part of hypocrites – got no use fer 'em 'tall. That's the main reason he don't go ta church much. Pa an' Ma say prayers an' sometimes we read the Bible but that's 'bout it."

Mel smiled as he examined little Bill's gunstock.

"Think you can fix that busted wood, Mr. Mel?"

"I was just thinkin' whether to completely break this stock into two pieces or to repair it as it is."

"If you break it into two pieces, isn't that worse?"

"Well, Pumpkin, sometimes somethin' or someone has to totally break before they can be fixed properly. Once I clean this up, I want to glue an' clamp it so the crack looks like a line of grain in the wood. I want to give it the appearance of a brand new stock."

"I was thinkin' he was pretty particular 'bout what he did – right down ta the way he drank sweet tea! He didn't gulp it, didn't sip it. He'd take the one drink, put the glass down an' enjoy that one mouthful of cool pleasure. I watched him that afternoon take that splintered piece of wood an' started repairin' it in a carin' an' almost lovin' way. He gently took his hand tools an' cleaned the two pieces of wood so that they fit together in a seamless fashion. Once he finished that, he glued an' clamped the wood together."

"Well, that needs to set fer the night," Mel said.

"What else do you haf'ta do?" I asked.

"Well, tomorrow either your pa or I will sand'n the stock down an' put a little finish on it. If I'm here, I'll checker that fore grip to help hide the seam, so little Bill can git a better grip on it."

"There wasn't no 'lectricity in the shed an' it was gittin' into in the day. As Mel finished wipin' up the excess glue, Pa walked into the shed's doorway. Mel showed Pa the stock. Pa's not a man ta say thin's he didn't mean."

"Mel, you did a better job than I would've. I guess you were some really fine cabinet maker, huh?"

"Well, I enjoy workin' with wood an' well, it's just a God-given gift."

"Pa was impressed. I didn't see Pa impressed much, so it always made me pay attention when he was studyin' on somethin'. Once a man in town carved a 36-inch link of wooden chain from a single piece of wood. It impressed Pa, not just the carvin' but the patience an' thought that went into doin' it. "Another time I saw Pa impressed was when one of the colored-men down the road from us caught himself a catfish that weighed over 100 pounds. He stopped on his way home an' called Pa ta look at what he had in the back of his wagon. Pa said that was the biggest fish he ever saw an' couldn't believe that ol' boy was able ta catch it without bein' drowned. So when Pa asked Mel ta finish the work on the stock the next day, I knew Pa was pretty impressed."

"Now, where you be spendin' the night?" Pa asked.

"Oh, just down the way a piece. I'll be back in the mornin'," Mel said.

"Well, if it ain't a lot o' trouble. I don't want to be puttin' you out or changin' your plans."

What Pa was really sayin' was he didn't want ta be beholdin' ta a stranger. Pa just kinda liked Mel right off. I think that bothered him a bit – that just wasn't like Pa."

"Hey, y'all! Come in an' wash up!" Momma yelled. "Suppertime!"

"Boy, I 'member my Pa was a bit flustered. I think he was thinkin' he should invite Mel fer supper, but he didn't know him. Pa kinda stood there like my first beau – kinda not knowin' what ta do, so doin' nothin'."

Mel spoke up. "I'll see y'all in the mornin' an' finish this up fer the day," he said as he gently laid the stock on the bench, an' he walked off as quick as he came.

"Pa, you should've asked him ta supper!" I said.

"Go git washed up!" he snapped.

"I know he knew I was right. He always got a little mad when he didn't do what he felt he should but did what he oughtta do. An' if Momma or me or little Bill suggested he shoulda done it – whoa – we'd git a look!" Grammy smiled at the face of her father imprinted on her memory. "I really think that look was fer him an' not fer us," she concluded.

"I 'member sittin' at the table that night. Momma asked, "Otis, where's he from?"

"I don't know," Pa said.

"Where's he goin'?"

"Don't know that either."

"Does he have any kin 'round here?"

"Annie! I just don't know nothin'!" Pa said.

That made me an' little Bill start ta giggle, an' then Momma joined in. We all tried ta keep respectful an' all, but it just tickled us ta hear Pa sayin' he didn't know nothin'. Pa finally smiled an' gave a little chuckle. He took my ma's hand an' said, "I knew enough ta marry you."

"Then I guess you're sayin' I didn't know nothin'," Ma teased, an' we all laughed so hard. I thought the whole world was jealous that they weren't sittin' 'round our table that night.

Chapter 2

The next mornin', I heard deep voices outside. My window looked onta the back of the house. I could see the barn in our yard area, two of the cottonwood trees an' the woods. Every mornin', the sun would come up over those trees. Usually, I would wake ta hear the gruntin' an' squealin' of pigs or the cluckin' of some hens, but this mornin' Pa was talkin' ta someone – Mel! I jumped up an' ran downstairs in my nightshirt. When I got ta the kitchen, Pa an' Mel were walkin' in. Pa asked Mel ta take breakfast with him. Momma had the coffee on an' some side bacon poppin' in the skillet.

"Good Mornin', Pumpkin," Mel said ta me.

"Mornin, Mel," I replied.

"Child," Momma corrected, "Mr. Mel."

Momma was always a stickler fer bein' proper, polite an' all. It was always "Hello, Miss Melba" or "Good-bye, Mr. Roy."

"Annie this is Mel..."

"Just Mel, Ma'am. I met your two young'uns in

the woods yesterday an' Otis here when I walked 'em home. It's a pleasure ta make your acquaintance."

"It's a pleasure ta meet you, Mel. Please have a seat; breakfast will be done shortly."

I sat an' watched the men eat breakfast. I had some toast an' milk. I always stirred a little honey in my milk. Pa was tellin' Mel 'bout the cotton fields he was workin'. There was a threat of bollweavels ruinin' the crop this year an' Pa was doin' everythin' in the fields ta prevent 'em insects ta come in an' destroy all his hard work.

"Do you 'member the cotton fields?"

"Yes, Grammy, I do."

"They seemed to go on forever when I was a child," she recollected. They'd go straight out to the north an' east of our property. As you stood in the front of the house, a patch of field was ta the west, almost out ta over where those ponds were, across the road, ta the west a bit, the old Prichert property.

"Didn't one of those ponds have an alligator in it?" he asked.

"Yes, it did – fer years, 'til Uncle Joe caught an' kilt it. It was a big one, over ten feet long. Pa took me ta the ponds a lot growin' up, ta catch bream an' bass, we talked a lot there as we walk 'round those banks."

"Anyways," she went on, "at breakfast, Pa asked Mel if he was goin' ta stayin' 'round a while or movin' on. I waited, wide-eyed with my breath held. I really didn't know him, but havin' company 'round was always fun. An' he was so nice."

"Well, I was thinkin' last night 'bout spendin' a little time in these parts, that's if I could be a help to someone, maybe find a little work."

Pa carefully picked his words, not ta pry or commit anythin' ta Mel. "Well, I might could use some help here, an' I know the mill always could use a strong back," Pa offered.

Mel smiled an' swallowed a bit of eggs an' toast.

"I'm not lookin' fer a regular job. I just would like to help if you could use me awhile."

Pa was kinda perplexed – he would never take somethin' fer nothin' – he didn't have much money. We pretty much grew all our food an' traded fer other stuff. Pa called it a garden, but we could feed five families off our crops. Made a lot of hoe'n fer little Bill an' me. I don't think Momma owned a store-bought dress an' I always felt guilty when I grew a little, an' my clothes would git tight. Mel continued after a swallow of his black coffee.

"You prob'ly have a load o' work 'round here fixin' or repairin' an with workin' in the fields takes a lot o' daylight to git the jobs done. If you want I'll help you. I'll help by, well, by mendin' your fence by the pig trough. I noticed the chicken coop roof needs some attention. Oh, I'm sure you an' your missus could keep me busy fer a time."

Pa sat there thinkin' what ta do. What could he give Mel? Mel knew Pa didn't have a clue on strikin' a bargain, an' he wanted ta put Pa at ease."

"How 'bout this?" Mel suggested. "How's 'bout you let me clean up the shed, an' I sleep in there. I can take meals with your family." Then turnin' to Ma, "an' maybe you, Annie, could make me a shirt outta some cloth I have?"

I was thinkin' Pa thought Mel was stupid. We always had plenty ta eat. Momma was the best gardener in the whole county. I think she was the best cook, too. She canned everythin' from goobers ta chowchow relish, an' could make a shirt with her eyes closed. Pa sat there lookin' at Mel.

"Well, I could pay ya a bit o' money fer a few weeks."

Now, I'm thinkin' – Pa, he didn't ask fer money! Don't give away money if'n someone doesn't ask fer it! Pa just wasn't dealin' too good.

"I'm really not here lookin' fer much money," Mel told Pa. "I could use a shirt made. Annie's food is the best I've had in a long time an' I'd find pleasure in workin' an' helpin' with some o' those repairs. A man always feels better at night havin' worked hard durin' the day. Who knows? Maybe after I prove I can fix a thin' or two, some people you know might need some help an' I could pick up some odd chores fer 'em. If I happen to stay 'round here awhile. Then you can say, 'He did a good job fer me!' A man's gotta prove his salt, this would be the best way fer me, that is, if you're willin' to help me."

"Well," I thought, "that cuts it. He is stupid. He's gonna work like a mule fer food an' a shirt an' a dirty old shed an' Pa will be a helpin' him if'n he lets him do it! I still liked Mel, I knew he was special, but he was a worse bargainer than Pa!"

"I once traded two frogs an' a snappin' turtle ta the Redden brothers fer two Indian arrowheads an' a piece of yellow yarn," the old woman chuckled through a rattling chest cough. "I'm sure the frogs an' turtle are dead, maybe even the Redden boys, but I still have those arrowheads."

The boy smiled at the financial wizardry that his dear grandmother displayed at such a tender age.

"I 'member Momma lookin' at Pa sayin' with her eyes, "If he wants ta work let him work!"

There was always somethin' ta do on the farm. The deal was struck an' Mel thanked Momma fer the breakfast, excused himself an' said he was gonna finish little Bill's gun so he could git ta work.

"Young lady," Ma called, "Go on with your chores, it's gittin' late. An' wake up little Bill."

I walked inta little Bill's room. He was sleepin' in his little feather bed. I watched his chest rise an' fall with each breath. A small voice inside me said, "Thank you, God, fer my baby brother."

Then I hit him in the head with my pillow an' yelled, "Git up you lazy bones! We got critters ta feed an' taters ta water an' I can't do it by myself! I hit him a couple more times fer good measure – he was always a hard one ta wake up."

She smiled at her boy sitting on the hospital bed next to her. "I 'member throwin' water on you a time or two!"

He smiled and turned to the table behind him, sticking his finger in the water pitcher. He playfully dabbed the wet digit on the tip of the old woman's nose.

"Gotcha back," he quipped.

She placed her warm bony hand over his. "Let me finish my story," she continued. "That first day Mel finished little Bill's gun, sandin' an' oilin' it up, an' puttin' it back together. I couldn't even see where it was broke. Mel even added a little engravin' design 'round here an' there. Pa was mighty impressed by Mel's craftsmanship. Mel started helpin' Pa 'round the farm. I 'member goin' ta school an' wishin' I was home ta help Mel, if'n he needed me. I was more in the way than helpful, but Mel never let on. That first week he was there, he got all sorts of chores done. I was worried he finished everythin' an' would be on his way. Little did I know! Mel was bein' a big help ta Pa mendin' fences, doin' some leatherwork on the harnesses, he even got up on the roof ta fix some shingles Pa kept promisin' ta repair, an' would ferget 'til it'd rain. Then he'd curse the weather, not enough time in a day, an' everythin' else that needed doin' an' was still broke."

"I 'member that first Sunday mornin' I woke up early ta hear Pa out back talkin' ta Mel.

"So will you be joinin' your family to meetin' this mornin?" Mel asked.

"No, God could afford ta take off on the Sabbath – I can't." Pa replied.

"When do you take time ta rest your body an' soul?"

Pa just looked at Mel. Mel just went on. "You see, I think God was pretty smart, settin' one day aside to rest, enjoin' life, kinda focusin' on Him an' all He's blessed us with."

"You a preacher, too?" Pa asked.

"No, just one who's thankful – thankful God cared enough to bother with me, love me, even showed me how ta take a day an' rest." Mel smiled.

"I guess you'll be goin' ta meetin," Pa said.

Mel smiled. "Wouldn't miss it."

The Reverend Blanchard was surprised to see us walk in with a man not our pa.

"Who do we have here?"

Mel extended his hand. "My name's Mel. I'm workin' out at the Gilbert's, helpin' Otis with some odd jobs."

"Well, it's great ta have you here this mornin'. Tell Otis I missed him." The reverend always said that.

"I will. Maybe he'll be out meetin' here one o' these Sundays!"

The reverend smiled an' gave Mel 'the eye,' meanin' 'I'll believe it when I see it!'

We sat by My Aunt Lee an' Uncle Joe, as we did every Sunday. My cousins Janey, an' Dorothy fidgeted next to me an' Billy week in an' week out.

"Good mornin', Annie, I see you finally up an' got yourself a new man. It's 'bout time."

"Joe T. Gilbert, you hush now before you go an' start stories you can't stop!" Ma whispered.

"Mel, this is Joe an' Lee Gilbert, Otis' brother." Momma introduced.

"Nice ta meet you," Uncle Joe greeted the stranger.

"I think Otis hired you on so maybe no one woulda noticed he was never here."

"Otis asked Mel ta stay on with us a bit an' help with some work that needs doin'."

Aunt Lee nodded at Mel an' the service started. I 'member sittin' next ta Mel. He knew all the words ta ev'ry hymn. He was so respectful of the service. It was the first time I think I understood that we were here ta worship. Mel had his own Bible, an' when he opened it I could tell he read it a lot. He even wrote in it an' underlined passages. He studied it hard! When Mel bowed his head fer prayer, I heard him whisper, "Yes, Jesus. Thank you, Jesus."

It made me feel good, kinda safe. I kinda wished my Pa was more like Mel. There was the after church visitin', people makin' their way through the circles o' conversation greetin' each other, passin' on bits an' pieces of news, an' chitchat. Mel had many introductions made, an' he seemed ta be quite the center o' interest. On the way home, Billy held Momma's hand an' I held Mel's. That road was always dusty, but that Sunday, I didn't mind much.

"Mel," Momma started, "where 'bouts are your people from?"

"Oh, I knows folks all over, but mainly back east."

"What brings you south?"

"Well, I hadn't been ta this part o' the country an' I just had the need."

"What do you think?" Momma asked.

"This time of year seems real pretty, an' I like the people!" Mel swung my arm up high.

"How long you plannin' on stayin' in these parts?" Momma asked.

"Well, I'm makin' my way out to see the redwoods

on the west coast," Mel explained. "But I'm goin' ta enjoy the journey." He smiled as the warm dusty air blew across the road. "It's always nice to get where you're goin', but it's how you make the journey that's important!"

"Momma," Billy whined. "What's fer supper?"

"Well, I'm gonna fry up some chicken an' okra, mash some potatoes an' cook some beans. You'll be takin' supper with us, Mel," Annie said. It wasn't a question.

"Thank you," Mel smiled an' raised his eyebrows, his brown an' green eye twinklin'.

I saw Pa aways off an' it bothered me he was a watchin' us come home from church. I was wishin' he was walkin' with us. I squeezed Mel's hand a little harder. When we got ta the edge of our yard Billy an' I ran ta Pa. "You should have been there," I said. "The sermon was 'bout God harvestin' his fields, kinda like us with the cotton."

"I'm sure he has a lot of new-fangled equipment," Pa replied, as he wiped the evidence of mornin' chores from his brow.

"No," Mel said as he approached the conversation. "He harvests one cotton ball at a time."

"I'm startin' supper," Momma called. "Don't stray far."

"Pastor missed you at meetin' today," Mel commented.

"Yeah, well I get there when I can," Otis replied.

"I think those young'uns miss you the most."

Pa looked at Mel firmly. Mel was treadin' in places he ought not be. Otis' silence spoke clearly, that maybe Mel should make his observances in silence, too. Otis continued to wipe the sweat off the back of his neck.

"You have any plans fer this afternoon?" he asked.

"No, I can't say that I do,' Mel replied.

"My brothers, Johnny an' Joe, an' a couple of the boys are goin' fishin' fer cats down at the river. If'n you wanna come, we're leavin' after lunch.'

"I'd like that. I'd like that a lot. But I don't have a pole."

Otis smiled. "You've got everythin' you need."

Chapter 3

Supper was pleasant. Lotsa laughter an' good food. Mel an' Pa were on the front porch waitin' fer Uncle Joe ta pick 'em up.

"Eula, Bill, come here!" Pa yelled.

I looked at Momma. She nodded in the direction of Pa.

"Go see what your Pa needs, Child."

I put down my dryin' cloth an' hurried out ta the front porch. Little Bill was already there.

"You two wanna go ta the river?" Pa asked.

Billy an' I were so excited. "Oh, yes, Pa, yes!"

"Tell your ma Jane an' Dorothy are goin' too.

Jane an' Dorothy were my best friends growin' up. We children had a special job when we went fishin'. We would take care o' the catch. We'd put 'em in an old burlap bag an' tote 'em 'round. Those fish would jump an' roll 'round in that sack. When the men were done an' ready ta clean the fish all the fish goo an' slime would be wiped off inside o' the bag. Pretty smart!

Soon Uncle Joe's wagon was in front of the house. Their dappled, gray mare, Lucille, pulled it. The girls were in the back. Little Bill an' I climbed in an' started ta giggle. We were off ta the river. In those days the ride ta where you were goin' was almost as important as the destination. It was always bumpy, dusty an' loud.

"You children settle down a bit. You're gettin' on Lucille's nerves."

Uncle Joe would make that claim a dozen times before we would get ta the river. He was a bit of a barker, but he never bit us, even though he had a reputation of bein' the county scrapper. It was said he once busted out the front two teeth of a man an' broke his nose with one punch, all 'cause the man told him ta hurry up. I guess Uncle Joe was just never in a hurry.

We finally got ta the river an' there was my Uncle Johnny an' Mr. Roy an' Mr. Homer. They all grew up together in this county an' had been fishin' an' huntin' together since childhood." Now, Uncle Johnny took after the Brewer side of the family. He was short, round, an' always had a smile. He worked fer the railroad fer forty-two years. Mr. Roy had been Pa's best friend growin' up. He was tall an' thin. He worked in town fer the bank. I don't 'member Mr. Homer too well. He was real quiet. His hand had been crushed when he was a young man.

It had bunched up his knuckles. I guess kids notice thin's like that.

"Hey y'all!' Pa greeted. "This is Mel; he's been helpin' out at our place."

"Mel, you went ta the right farm. Otis needs all the help he can git."

Mr. Roy joked. "It'll take the burden off us, havin' ta help him all these years."

"Yes sir, he's one bit o' sorry," Uncle Johnny threw in. Mr. Homer an' Mr. Roy just laughed at the abuse Pa was takin'.

"Boys," Pa slowly began, "Mel here has never been grabbin' before."

"Grabbin?" Mel repeated. "I thought we were fishin'?"

"Mel, grabbin' is a form of fishin. It's how men fished before there was cane poles an' fish line."

"All the men were lookin at Mel an' smilin'."

"This is fishin' - real fishin," Mr. Homer explained. "Ya gotta git in ta the water an' walk along the bank.'

"In your bare feet," Uncle Johnny added. "Then you feel your way along the bank edge where the river cuts into it. You search those nooks an' crannies, look fer holes anywhere a cat would like to hold up."

"Keep an eye out fer fall downs an' log jams!" Mr. Roy added.

Mr. Homer looked 'round at everyone impatiently. "Am I explainin' this or not?"

"Go on, Homer, an' feel free ta take your time," Roy jabbed.

Mel was still tryin' ta wrap his brain 'round this gittin in the water thin'.

"Ya find the fish by stickin' your toe into one of those crevices an' feelin' the cat just lyin' there."

"You boys are just joshin' me," Mel hoped.

Their faces revealed the horrible truth - Mel was gittin' wet.

"Once you find the cat," Mr. Homer started, raisin' his voice a bit, "let us know an' move real slow like – don't want ta spook it. The closest man ta you will come over an' stand by the hole ta block it so it can't swim out. That's when you reach in an' grab it by the mouth. Take a good holt of him, let 'em bite down hard."

"Then what?" Mel asked.

"Then you just hang on tight, drag him out of his home an' toss 'em up on shore," Pa finished the lesson.

"The young'uns will bag the fish."

Mel stood there, still a bit in disbelief. Uncle Joe was rollin' up his pant legs, an' easin' himself into the current.

"Come on, Mel, it's time fer your baptism."

"They started slowly workin' the river upstream.

Their toes were their guides ta the prey they sought. It was a sunny day, the catfish would be holdin' ta the bank an' deep holes in the river. We grabbed the ol' potato sack an' started ta follow the brave men, keepin' back aways from the bank, an' at a distance as not ta spook the fish. All the men were up ta their knees an' thighs in the river. Mel kept lookin' 'round, I guess waitin' fer the joke ta be over.

"Now, Mel, you make sure it's a cat you be a grabbin," Uncle Joe warned. "You don't want ta be surprisin' a snappin' turtle or a cottonmouth."

"Turtle'll take your fin'er clean off," Mr. Homer acknowledged as he raised his left hand, displayin' a missin' digit. "Cottonmouths will just make you sick."

"Now Homer, you didn't lose that finger fishin'!" Pa said.

"Otis, he didn't know that!" Mr. Homer complained. "I had a good thing goin' there an' you ruined it. That turtle would've been 60 pounds by the time that story was finished."

"Snakes? I don't like snakes," Mel stated. "I find 'em ta be vile creatures. With little or no redeemin' worth."

"Whoaaa, watch out! Snake!' Uncle Johnny threw a crooked branch in Mel's general direction. "I come close ta losin' this fin'er when I was little Bill's age."

"That would've been a sin," Mr. Homer chirped in. "That's the one he uses ta pick his nose with."

We kids just laughed. It was always fun ta hear grown-ups tease each other. We kept pace with the men up on the bank. We walked through the tall blown down grass. This was my favorite stretch o' river. We had many a picnic along here. Old willows an' cottonwoods lined the river an' the maiden grass laid heavy over the bank into the movin' water. We could make crowns an' necklaces out of the wildflowers while we waited fer flyin' fish. I could've spent every day o' my childhood there.

"Got one!" Pa yelled. He didn't wait fer help. He dropped ta his knees. Uncle Johnny waded over ta help. He reached up under the bank. The water started ta boil. Mel stood there takin' it all in. Pa pulled out a good cat. His arm was jerkin' like he'd been hit by a lightnin' bolt. Water was everywhere.

"Hang on!" Uncle Joe hollered.

"Get 'im, Otis!" yelled Mr. Roy.

"It's a baby. Throw 'im back," teased Mr. Homer.

Pa grabbed his wrist an' swung the big cat up on the bank. We raced ta jump on it an' put it in the bag. The men just stood there a second, admirin' Pa's catch, the way men do.

"Honestly, I thought y'all was kiddin'.... I don't know if I really want to do this," I heard Mel say.

"Well, that's how it's done," Pa said as he washed

his bloody knuckles off in the river.

"The lesson's over, Mel. You go 'head an' take the lead."

Uncle Johnny stepped aside ta make way fer the greenhorn ta take his turn. I could see Mel wasn't quite sure this is what he wanted ta be doin' on a Sunday afternoon, but choices had been made. Mel slowly moved along the river's edge, same as Pa, movin' out one foot, then the other, searchin' out under the murky mystery. Mel looked like a man tryin' ta walk a picket fence. His arms out straight, catty wampus, ta keep his balance. He was intent on findin' a cat an' keepin' his toes intact.

"Come on, Mel, show Otis how it's really done," Mr. Roy encouraged.

"Hey . . .I think I've found one!" Mel hollered.

"Pa rushed ta his side. "Okay, we got 'im blocked. You reach down an' work your hand over him gently, 'til you find his mouth. Then you grab 'im by his lower jaw an' hang on."

Mel looked at Pa as if he was wearin' Momma's best dress an' hat.

"Do what?" Mel questioned

"Get ta it, boy," Pa said.

Mel bent over an' stuck both his arms up ta their pits beneath that muddy water. He was feelin' 'round an' kept blowin' the grass from the bank out of his face. Mel's face went under the water a couple o' times, the deeper he dug. All the men were watchin' the greenhorn an' enjoyin' the show!

"Got 'em! Got 'em!" yelled Mel.

He slipped on the muddy bottom an' went ta one knee. The fish was twistin' an' flashin.' Mel had one hand in his mouth an' fer some reason was tryin' ta grab the tail with the other.

"Get 'em!" yelled Uncle Joe.

"Hang on!" laughed Mr. Roy.

I don't think Mel heard anythin'.

"I don't know who's got who," Pa said.

All the men were laughin' an' Mel was now down on both knees. His whole hand was in the cat's mouth an' the cat was rollin'! Mel's wrist was gettin'' chewed! Mel tried ta stand but he lost his footin' an' sprawled out face down in the river. The men hooted. Mel scrambled ta his feet, fish in hand. Pa reached out an' grabbed the fish, an' Mel an' gave 'em both a toss t'wards shore. The fish landed a few feet from the edge o' the water, but little Bill was on it.

"Pa, it's bigger than yours!" Bill yelled.

"I'll eat good," said Pa.

Mel was out o' breath. He plunked himself on the bank then slid off inta the water. He was up ta his chest, sittin' in the river. Everyone was hootin' an' hollerin'! This was the best fishin' day ever!

"Come on, Mel," Pa said. "We got lots o' mouths

ta feed." Pa gave Mel a hand up.

"Well, if I knew what a good time this was I'd stayed back at the farm an' worked on the roof," Mel laughed.

The men worked their way up the bank on one side an' down the other. We caught 16 fish that day. After we kids played in the water, it was time ta go home. We said our good-byes. All the men seemed ta like Mel. I sat up front on the ride home an' listened ta Mel, Pa an' Uncle Joe talk.

"You did better than most, first time out," Pa complimented Mel.

"Well, all I did was hang on – the fish did the rest," Mel explained with a chuckle.

Mel looked back at the kids who were lookin' in the bag of fish an' gave me a wink an' a smile.

"You two boys are truly blessed," Mel said lookin' at Pa an' Uncle Joe.

"You're invited back ta my place. The coop needs cleanin' an' I'd be happy ta share those blessin's with you," Uncle Joe said.

Pa laughed. Mel grinned.

Mel continued, "You both have good families an' strong, healthy kids. That's a blessin'."

"You're right, Mel," Pa broke in quietly. "We have healthy children, an' that is everythin'. The pain in losin' a child, well, it changes you, I couldn't bear that grief ...." his voice trailed off ta silence.

I knew Pa loved us, I never heard him say he worried 'bout us. I thought of how close little Bill come ta killin' himself. That would be a terrible pain.

"'Member Calvin Johnson? He never was the same after he lost his boy," Uncle Joe said; as soon as the words left his mouth, he looked at Pa. An awkward silence replaced the conversation. Pa nodded quietly. They both looked down the road ahead.

"So, how long you two been brothers?" Mel asked.

Uncle Joe started laughin'. "At times, a lot longer than I'd like!"

"Which times are those, Joe? The time I saved your bacon from the Henry brothers? Or maybe that time I told your wife you was with me, when you really was playin' cards at Turner's!"

Pa raised his eyebrows an' voice with a tone of 'I dare you.'

"Hey, little pitchers have big ears!" Uncle Joe cautioned as he looked in my direction.

Mel smiled.

"Family secrets is a treasure chest with many keys," Mel noted.

Men have a way of keepin' each other in check with shame an' threats an' 'memberin' each other's past weaknesses, 'specially brothers. After all these years . . . I 'member that ride home an' the supper table that night. Mel spoke o' mountains an' oceans, big cities an' people he met along the way. It seemed Mel knew somethin' 'bout most everythin', not in an uppity kinda way, just, well, experience.

"Mel, have you ever been married?" Ma asked.

"No, no I haven't."

Momma wanted ta ask more, like me. But it wasn't polite. Mel would make a great husband if he wasn't movin' 'round so much. Maybe he could find someone round here. I began ta think hard. There was Miss Melba an' Miss Flo, both of whom were gettin' on up close ta their twenties. There was the widow Hawkins, she had two young'uns. Mel would make a great Pa, too! An' she was still pretty,

"I don't believe I'll ever settle down Annie," Mel explained. "It seems my shoes were made ta wander."

"Well that cuts it," I thought. Hitchin' Mel would be pretty near impossible if he wasn't gonna stick 'round.

"Momma," I darted inta the conversation.

"Yes, Child."

"Did you see Miss Melba's dress at meetin' today?"

"I didn't notice it, Hon," Annie replied.

"Well, it was white with a little sprin' flower pattern all over it. She looked so pretty. Mr. Mel, did you see Miss Melba? She sat three pews in front of us an' ta the left."

"I'm sorry, Pumpkin, I didn't notice," Mel apologized.

'DIDN"T NOTICE!?' I thought. 'Either he's as blind as a bat. ...or maybe, just maybe, he's as sly as a fox. I bet he noticed. Just bidin' his time. OR, maybe he didn't care fer the color o' Miss Melba's hair or somethin'. Her hair was auburn, she was on the thin side, an' her complexion was so fair.... that's it! Mel doesn't care fer dark haired, skinny, pasty lookin' girls,' I concluded. Now Miss Flo had blonde hair, an' the sun had licked her skin golden brown.

"Momma," I once again inquired. "Did you see Miss Flo today?"

"Yes, Baby, I did. She was sittin' next ta that young Mr. McRoberts."

'Oh Momma,' I thought, 'Don't be makin' it sound like that big-eared boy could raise Miss Flo's biscuits, let alone her interest.' If'n Mel thought Miss Flo was spoken fer he'd never speak ta her in a social way. Mel wasn't a sort ta bust in on someone else's gal.

"I'm sure Mr. McRoberts isn't courtin' Miss Flo," I started, all the time lookin' at Mel.

"She's just a peach of a girl who'd befriend a mouse if'n she was a piece of cheese." Mel smiled.

"Eula Mae," Pa said, catchin' on ta where the conversation was goin'.

"Pa, I'm just sayin' Miss Flo is one o' the most sweetest single ladies in the whole county."

"Eula! Don't be pokin' your nose where it ought not be!"

My pa didn't like ta chew his cabbage twice. When he wanted the conversation dropped, it needed ta fall in the sea's deepest abyss.

"Eula, you can help me with these dishes."

"Yes, Ma'am." I went on an' cleared the table.

Pa an' Mel was talkin' fishin.' Little Bill was playin' in the livin' room.

"Mel, did you hear 'bout the Germans sinkin' that ship - the Lusitania?"

"No, I hadn't heard."

"There were over 1100 people on board, more than 100 were Americans. We'll be in this fight before ya know it."

"War is such an ugly condition ta which man has resigned himself ta settlin' his differences," Mel sadly commented.

"You don't think we oughta join in an' fight those @#%@&* aggressive Hinney warmongers ?" Pa explored with a bit of vim an' viger.

"Otis!" Momma called sharply. "The children!"

Like we never heard Pa sling a slew o' swears before. Like that time when Oscar, our hog, trampled

Pa down an' bit 'im. That string of swears was heard all the way ta town!

"Sorry, Annie, but they are one aggressive people. Now they're killin' civilians on the high seas - nothin' more than pirates," Pa muttered.

"America will join the war, eventually. That's what men an' countries do. Always with the hope an' prayer that the result will be everlastin' peace." Mel witnessed.

Pa thought a moment. "There was this old soldier's home out on the other side o' town when I was a kid. Those men were always millin' 'round, or just sittin' on the porch watchin' the comin's an' goin's of the town. They kept ta themselves a lot. Seemed friendly enough, just a bit odd. I guess war does that ta a man," Pa 'membered.

"It seems that in every conflict, there's a search fer peace," Mel observed.

Little Bill ran through the house chasin' an invisible adversary an' hollerin' in tongues.

"Hush boy, go on outside with that noise," Pa called out. "I'd like some peace myself," he chuckled ta Mel.

Pa seemed at ease with Mel, almost like he was kin. He was a lot nicer ta folks after he met Mel.

"I found a peace a long time ago," Mel said softly, catchin' Pa's attention. Mel went on. "A peace anyone can know. It comes from within at times when there should be no peace. It will replace fear, anger an' hopelessness."

"Ok, Mel, what're you sellin'?" Pa was always on the lookout fer the carpetbagger in everyone.

"Me? I've got nothin' to sell, I have a thing or two share, but money can't pay fer 'em," Mel smiled at me as I put a glass away.

"A few winters back, I was up in the northern part o' Michigan. I was tryin' ta cross this lake that was froze over. I was takin' a short cut so I could make it ta a little town 'fore nightfall. It was a pretty area. You couldn't spit without hittin' a pine or spruce. I never noticed the ice gettin'' thin or rotten; it just gave way. An' quick as a bunny I was over my head in a very cold reality."

"Child, you're gonna wear that plate out if you dry it anymore," Momma said.

Mel went on. "I just hung there in the water, little bubbles floatin' upward toward the surface, but me an' all my truck just kinda hung there like a kite in the air. I began to kick my feet an' after what seemed like eternity, my head broke the surface. I was wearin' a hooded jacket an' the wind just whipped into that hood 'round my head an' froze my hair an' ears in a heartbeat. I splashed towards the ice. It just broke off in chunks as I tried to find some support before I slipped under the water again. I'll bet I broke up ten feet of ice before I found it thick enough to hold onto. All the while I'm thinkin even if I get out I'll freeze to death 'fore I get to town. I started to panic. I had to get out of the water. My whole body was goin' numb. I felt the strength drainin' from my fingers an' my arms. I clung to what I viewed as my savior, that shelf of ice. Then a passage of Scripture 'popped' into my head." Mel dramatized the word popped.

"I had been readin' in the book of Luke to not worry 'bout things in life. It wouldn't add a single day to your life. A peace washed over me an' warmed my soul, but not my toes. The Bible talks 'bout a God-given peace that passes understandin'. Just then, my foot bumped somethin'. It was a sunken stump or somethin'. I was able to rest a moment. I thanked God fer all He had blessed me with."

'Now, let's see,' I thought. 'In the middle of a frozen lake, up ta his armpits in ice water, an' he's countin' his blessin's.' I stole a look at Pa. He was listenin' hard to Mel's yarn.

"Then," Mel went on, "I felt someone pokin' me on the shoulder, right out there in the middle of the lake! Then I heard someone say, 'Let go of the ice.' I tried ta turn an' see who or what was behind me. My hood was froze, so no matter which way I spun my head the hood stood froze in place. 'Let go of the ice an' take ahold' is what I heard, so I let go with my right arm an' I come 'round a bit ta see a man an' boy layin' flat on the ice with a big ol' branch stickin' out ta me. I grabbed the branch an' they were able to haul me out of the water. They got me back to town an' took me home with 'em."

"William Johnson was a fine Christian, a deacon at the local church. He an' his wife, Sarah, took me in an' provided me with food, clothin' an' shelter all in the name of the Lord Jesus Christ."

Pa was silent.

"You know, Otis, I might never had met the Johnson's an' become friends had I not broke through the ice."

"How long did you stay there?" Pa asked.

"Well, the weather turned bad an' William was the shopkeeper in town – he had a general store. I stayed an' helped him out fer 'bout seven to eight weeks. You see, he had received a shipment of music boxes, most of which were damaged in shippin.' I was able to repair 'em. I did some engravin' on 'em to dress 'em up a bit. They turned out pretty nice. He sold most of 'em before I left."

"I heard God works in mysterious ways," Pa said.

"You know, boy," the old woman said to her grandson as he sat beside her in the hospital, "low those many years ago, I never fergot how God provides. You'd think fallin' through the ice would be a bad thing. God can take a bad situation an' use it ta His glory, ta His purpose. I often wondered if

Mel thought God was tappin' at his shoulder when Mr. Johnson was pokin' him with that stick," the old woman chuckled at the thought. Her memories continued to unravel. I 'member Mel thankin' Momma fer dinner an' Pa fer the day fishin.'

"Mel, you surely must like water - even today you was up ta your waist in it more than once!" Pa laughed.

I wished Pa would share a story kinda like make hisself a little easier to understand'n. Mel just seemed so open, not afraid what people thought. You'd always know if Pa was mad or tickled. I had never known if he was scared or sad or felt deep 'bout a subject. I had not 'membered the last time Pa had told any of us he loved us. I knew he did 'cause Momma always told us. I guess I was just growin' up a bit an' wanted a deeper an' closer relationship with my pa. Just didn't know how ta go 'bout it.

Chapter 4

Little Bill an' I were off ta school the next day. Mel was on the wagon replacin' some boards. Pa was walkin' the field. Momma was as always in the kitchen.

"Bye, Pa!" little Bill hollered an' waved. Pa waved back.

Little Bill had a ritual every mornin' on the way ta school. He'd throw rocks. He'd throw 'em at trees, fence posts, birds, other kids – he just was a rock thrower. This mornin' was no different. We met up with Jane an' Dorothy down the road. Janey was a lot like me. She could find the sun on a cloudy day. Now, Dorothy, she liked cloudy days, an' was a very thoughtful soul. Soon a troop of us were standin' out front o' the schoolhouse. Jane an' Dorothy wanted ta know all 'bout Mel an' I just had ta tell 'em. Little Bill was still throwin' stones. Now I didn't see it, but Tommy Watkins said Bill threw a stone at him. I got over there quick an' Tommy was pushin' little Bill 'round in a circle.

"Hey, quit pushin' my little brother, you freckled-face toad!" I said.

That Watkins family had red hair an' a million freckles between 'em.

"He threw a stone at me!" Tommy shouted.

"Did he hit you?" I asked.

"No, but it was close!"

"If'n he was throwin' at you, he'd hit you 'cause he's an expert rock thrower!" I announced. "So just leave him alone, Tommy Watkins!"

"If he's so good, he could hit that tree over there!"

Before another squabble could git started, little Bill picked up a stone an' hit that tree square. The children on the schoolyard that day were all witnesses ta Little Bill's proficiency in the art of stone flingin'. He went up a notch in the peckin' order.

"Well, okay, but he'd better not throw any rocks at me, 'cause I'll bust his britches," Tommy threatened as he an' his friends moved along.

"Little Bill, don't you be gettin'' in trouble. I can't always be lookin' out fer you!"

"I didn't need your help," he huffed an' walked towards the tree he just hit.

"Come on, children. Classes are startin'!" Miss Dunham called.

She taught all the grades. I liked school. The more I learned, the more important I felt. I loved readin' my textbooks. I sometimes read 'em through two or three times. As we sat in class, Tommy Watkins was still givin' Little Bill dirty looks an' Bill returned 'em in spades. School days always seemed ta pass fast. I enjoyed spendin' the time with friends.

"Durn'in the week we had few visitors an' it was a time before 'overnights' your kids are used ta," the old woman reminded her boy.

When Miss Dunham dismissed us fer the day I was anxious ta git home an' see Mel.

Jane asked, "How long do you think he'll stay?"

"I was hopin' he'd get sweet on Miss Melba or Miss Flo," I said. "But he said he's a wanderin' man."

"That'd be a lonely life," Dorothy commented.

"Come on, Billy, keep up. We're not gonna be waitin' on you all day."

"Go on ahead; I'm stoppin' by the creek."

"You know Momma wants you ta come straight home."

"Don't you be tellin' on me, Eula!"

"If I heard that once, I heard it a thousand times," the old woman remembered.

I dropped the girls off at their road an' cut across the field fer home. As I got close, I saw Momma takin' down the wash. Mel an' Pa were workin' on takin out a big old hickory tree stump. One would chop it, thenthe other. I'm sure Momma had been pourin' ice tea all afternoon.

"Hey, Child," called Momma. "Where's your brother?"

"He was a tag-along. I think he's dawdlin' at the creek."

"That boy!" Pa complained. "He's got some chores ta do."

"He'll be along with the others," Momma assured. "How was your day, Honey?"

"It was good, I got a E on my spellin' words." This was the top grade.

"I could always spell," the old woman remembered.

Pa an' Mel were still takin' turns choppin' at that stump.

"How long you been workin' at this stump, Otis?" Mel asked.

"Off an' on fer maybe two years. I'll get it out one day." Pa promised.

"Girl, go throw some feed ta those chickens, not a lot," Pa instructed.

"Eula, do you have any homework? " Momma always asked that question like it was her after-school chore.

"No, Momma, not today; maybe little Bill does." That would make her ask him twice.

Pa an' Mel chopped away. I think Pa liked workin' that stump with Mel. A kinship at work at somethin' together.

"These roots will go deep," Mel said, wipin' the sweat from his brow.

"I've got a powder ta sprinkle on 'em. It's supposed ta dry the root out. Sprinkle, soak, an' shovel, cover the hole. That's the instructions."

"What you gonna do here; after the stump's gone?" Mel asked.

"I don't know; maybe I'll plant a tree," Pa laughed.

"I won't be here ta help you dig that stump out," Mel promised.

Pa looked at me. "Go ahead girl... the hens, take care of the hens."

"I'm goin,' Pa," I said as I jumped toward the coop.

" Heeeer chick, chick, chick, chick, chick. Heeeer, chick, chick, chick,"

I called the birds fer dinner. I filled their water pan, went an' fed the cats, an' gave 'em fresh water. Then I checked on a couple of mama pigs that had been penned off.

"Eula, put your books away. They're still sittin' out on the steps,"

Momma called. "An' where is that boy!"

Little Bill hadn't gotten home yet. "I'll check on him," I called as I run out of the house havin' put my books on my desk. I ran outside an' through the field. I saw a lone figure come up out of the woods from down by the creek. As I got closer, I saw little Bill kinda limpin' along. "Boy, if you don't hurry your gonna catch it. Momma an' Pa are . . . what happened ta you?"

He was all dirtied up, an' red-faced. He had been cryin', but he wasn't now. His hair was a mess an' his clothes were wet.

"That Tommy Watkins, Billy Watkins an' them LeFavour boys, Reid, Jake, an' Stoney followed me down by the creek. They pushed me in the water an' got my shoes all wet. When I got out, they pushed me in the dirt an' each took a turn sluggin' me."

"Those chicken-livered sissies, waitin' 'til you're all alone off in the woods. I'll get them tomorrow, just let 'em wait an' see," I vowed .

"No, I don't need your help. I'll get 'em," Little Bill said.

Now Momma always said I had a little bit of my Uncle Joe in me. The way she said it didn't make it sound like a good thin'. But I was gonna get those boys; I had a bit of a reputation of bein' able ta pop a boy in the jaw an' makin him cry, much ta Tommy Watkins embarrassment. None of 'em would go up against me either.

"Come on, we gotta tell Momma an' Pa."

"I don't want ta tell 'em. Momma will tell Pa ta go talk ta Mr.

Watkins an' that'll make thin's worst!"

"OK, but I won't be tellin' stories ta Pa or Momma. You're on your own."

Billy set his lower lip, an' was thinkin' all across the field of what ta say when he stood before the judgment throne waitin fer him at home. When little Bill saw Momma in the yard he let out a scream an' ran ta her. Momma put down her basket of wash an' ran out ta meet him. Now, Billy ran inta her arms cryin' an' sobbin' ta beat the band. I honestly don't know how he did it. Pa came over ta see what the commotion was all 'bout.

"Momma," wailed, "Maammaaa," He stuttered. I was really impressed. Mel stood at a distance lookin' on.

"What happened, Billy?" Momma asked.

"I was comin' home. An' I was tired so I dragged behind Eula Mae a bit an' she wouldn't wait up on me."

'Oh boy, yankin' me into this!' I thought.

"I was over by the covert at Thornapple Creek. I was lookin' down, just restin' fer a minute, an' a yellow jacket come buzzin' 'round my head. Then there was another, an' another. Oh, Momma, they was everywhere. I...I think there's a nest in those tall weeds. I kinda lost my footin', an' I slipped down the hill inta the creek. I think one stung me on the cheek, here," Billy pointed ta where one o' the cowards slugged him.

"Otis, it looks like the boy's been stung."

Pa took Billy by the chin an' turned his face ta the sun fer a better look. "It's kinda red," Pa studied.

"Come on, Billy, I'm takin' you in an' cleanin you up," Momma said like a mother hen, leavin' the wash in the yard.

"Eula, bring in the wash an' put it away while I tend your brother. An' you need ta wait on him comin' home from school. His little legs are shorter than yours."

Billy was real careful not ta look at me. 'Now if that that don't beat all,' I thought. 'I'm cleanin' up his mess.' The more I thought 'bout it, the angrier I got at those boys. I decided ta blame 'em fer me havin' ta put the wash away. Pa an' Mel went back ta choppin,' an' I got busy with the clothes. When I walked by little Bill sittin' at the table, I gave him a look. He knew he owed me big!

"Take some tea out ta Pa an' Mel. When I'm finished with Billy I gotta get the supper goin."

"Yes, Ma'am." I took out two big glasses. Mel leaned up against the stump an' somethin' caught Pa's eye by the fence, an' he took a walk ta investigate.

"That boy sure falls down a lot. Looked ta me like that hornet was 'bout this big," Mel said, makin' a fist. I don't know what overcame my bein', but I blurted out as so Pa couldn't hear. "Those Watkins

53

an' Lefavour boys beat up on little Bill, an' if'n Pa knows it, he'll just make it worst by goin over there."

"Do you think it's right to lie to your parents?" Mel asked.

"I didn't lie," I quickly protested. "Billy was the one runnin' the lie."

"Ohh," Mel seemed to understand.

"What's your part in all this goin' to be?" Mel questioned.

"I'm suspectin' I'm gonna have ta teach those boys ta leave my baby brother alone," I surmised.

"Now, how exactly would you do that? Is there a book you'd ask 'em ta read?" Mel pressed on.

"Well, I'd have 'em read the back of my hand an' the bottom of my foot," I announced, makin' sure Pa couldn't hear.

"Well, I'm sure that's the road Jesus would have followed. He would have called on 10,000 angels to set the score right," Mel said.

"Do you think?" I asked, wishin' Jesus would loan me a few angels ta take care o' the Thornapple Creek gang.

"No, Pumpkin, I don't think Jesus would do that. You see, Jesus was the most fergivin' man that ever lived. Why, on the cross, after the soldiers had beat Him an' mocked Him, an' even after they had spit on Him an' nailed his arms to the cross, He forgave 'em all."

"Fergave 'em? Why would he do that?" I asked.

"'Cause he loved 'em. That's the hardest kinda of love, lovin' those who don't love back," Mel concluded.

Now I had heard some silly thin's in my short time, but lovin' the Watkins boys was at the top of the heap.

"Pumpkin, fergiveness is a sign of strength, not weakness. Fergiveness just doesn't come natural. It's, well, evidence that Jesus is livin' in you."

"What happens if we go ta school tomorrow an' them boys figure on beatin' little Bill up again? Then do we put a hurtin' on 'em?

"Jesus was asked that same question once a long time ago. Now, Matthew, who was one of Jesus' disciples, was so impressed with the answer he wrote it down in his book."

"Well, how many times was it" I wanted a number, 'cause I could keep track of all them trespasses, then "POW" when they least expected it!

"The answer was seventy times seven."

I didn't know there was gonna be 'rithmetic; I wished I had a pencil an' paper ta figure the sum.

"How many is that, Mel?"

"How many do you think?"

"A lot."

"That's right, Pumpkin. Jesus wants us to fergive

those who hurt us, a lot."

Well, that kinda took the wind from my little sails. I was ready ta do battle an' now I'm bein' told a true warrior has gotta fergive. I thought Mel was a pretty smart man, so maybe I oughta think on what he said awhile . . . before I busted Tommy real good.

"Mel, please don't tell Pa what I told you," I asked

"Not my place, Pumpkin," Mel replied, seemin' to put it all on me.

"Eula Mae, come help get supper on the table," Momma called.

As I lay in bed that night, a war played out in my mind. On one side were these knights in black armor with drawn swords ready ta fight on the battlefield. I was with 'em, ready ta get back my little brother's honor that was taken from him that afternoon at the creek. On the other side were these gentle souls in white robes, nothin' ta protect themselves but the Bibles they held in their hands. It didn't seem fair, but somehow I felt the white robed soldiers were right. It was a fitful night tossin' back an' forth, I felt like I was wrestlin' with a mighty ferce. I woke up tired, with Mel's voice in my ear, 'Seventy times seven.' That had to be a mistake; no God would ask us ta keep fergivin.'

"Momma," I asked as I cut up my egg.

"Yes, Sweetheart."

"How many times does Jesus tell us ta fergive

someone?" Momma seemed pretty surprised at my biblical inquires. Billy looked up wonderin' what was goin' on.

"In the Bible, we are taught ta fergive all manners of trespasses."

"But does it tell us a number?"

"Well, Honey, Jesus said seventy times seven, which Pastor Blanchard interprets as 'any time you're needin' ta fergive someone,'" Momma explained.

I looked over at Billy ta see if he was gittin' all this. He was wolfin' down his eggs an' bacon. He was actin' like he was payin' no never mind ta what was bein' said.

In came Mel. "Mornin! Y'all sleep good?"

I'll bet he knew I had a terrible rest.

"I slept like a kitten," Eula said.

"Her purrin' kept me up," Billy laughed.

"Hurry children, Pa's comin' in fer breakfast an' you gotta get off ta school. Eula, why do you what ta know?"

"Never mind, Momma. I gotta git goin.' I can't be late. Bye, Momma, Bye, Mr. Mel!"

"Tell your Pa, eggs are gettin' cold. Mel's 'bout ta sit down."

I wanted ta skedaddle quick. No need fer Mel hearin' me askin' Momma 'bout fergivin' an' such.

"Bye, Pa," I called ta the barn.

"Bye, y'all be good!"

Little Bill an' I started off ta school. I was anxious ta see how the mornin' would play out.

"I'm gonna walk up ta Tommy Watkins an' bust him good," Billy said.

I looked at little Bill an' thought how yesterday I'd have slapped him on the back an' welcomed him ta manhood. But today, I'd been confused by all these notions Mel put in my head. Fergiveness, seventy times seven, love those who don't give a lick 'bout you! What's a body ta do with all that?

"Little Bill, you listen ta me good. You don't say a word ta Tommy or any of those others boys. Don't throw rocks by 'em, don't you even look at 'em."

"You aren't my ma."

"No, if'n I was, I'd beat your tail fer that fib you told yesterday," I assured.

"Eula, I owes Tommy... retribution fer hittin' on me yesterday."

"I'm thinkin' on somethin' an' you can't do nothin' 'til I'm done."

"Eula!" Billy protested.

"Hush!" I insisted.

We met up with the girls and explained what happen ta Billy yesterday an' how Billy didn't let on ta Momma an' Pa what really happened.

"Boy, there'll be a poundin' today!" Janey squealed

"I don't want ta get hit," Dorothy said

"Nobody's gonna git hit today. Mel was tellin' me how God set up the way fergivin' is suppose ta work. I'm not seein' the satisfaction in it, but I'm thinkin' it's the right way. So we just ignore old Tommy an' them other gooberheads. We'll act as if they don't exist."

Sure enough, we git ta school an' those boys were all lined up over by the swin'. That's where they hung. I never saw one of 'em in the swing'n, but that's where they stood, just ta be irritatin'. Billy, the girls and a few others were millin' 'round, talkin' 'bout this an' that. That's when I heard the catcallin'.

"I saw a baby fall in the water yesterday!" Tommy hollered, so his voice carried across the schoolyard.

"What kinda baby?" someone goaded.

"Oh, the kind that cries when they get thumped!"

All the boys started laughin' real obnoxious-like. Billy was gettin' madder an' madder. A nine-year-old boy's fuse is pretty short, an' Gilbert blood can cut that fuse in half.

"Billy," I steadied him, "'member we ain't doin' nothin'!"

"I wouldn't be at all surprised if those wet clothes that baby had on

weren't wet from the creek."   A lone voice marched across the grounds.

Laughter erupted from the swing. Janey grabbed Billy so he couldn't tear off inta that pack of name callers. The laughter started ta die down with every step I drew closer ta those boys. They kinda moved 'round so they could have a quick get-away or a better shot at hittin' me. I walked up ta within six feet of Tommy Watkins. I beckoned him with the twitch of my index fin'er. When he got close enough, I cupped my hand an' whispered in his ear, then I turned on my heel an' walked backed ta my friends. Tommy an' the boys stopped their tormentin' of Billy and us.

"What didja say ta that boy that would make him back off?" Janey asked.

"I told him if he didn't leave us alone, I was gonna ask Miss Dunham if she'd be so kind as ta ask Tommy's pa ta tell Tommy ta stop kissin' me all the time."

"Oh, Eula, you told a lie!" Dorothy cooed.

"No! I told him I would tell a lie," I corrected.

This fergiveness stuff was gonna take some time ta figure out. I was gonna make some mistakes along the way. I didn't exactly fergive Tommy that day, but I didn't hit him either. He could thank Mel fer that. When we got home that day. Mel greeted us in the front yard. Little Bill said 'Hi' an' ran inta the house ta find somethin' ta fill the hole in his belly.

"Anybody at school get a bloody nose today?" Mel asked.

I just giggled. "No," I answered.

"Black-eye, fat lip? " he continued in a surprised tone.

"Not that I know of, or had anythin' ta do with," I swore.

" Were all those boys sick at home today?" Mel kept on with the questions.

"They were all there," I assured. "I just sorta fergave 'em. Well... I didn't hit 'em. It's a start!"

Mel smiled. "That it is, an' every journey has to start somewhere.

Today it was with Tommy Watkins!"

I went inside an' Momma asked how my day was, and if I had any homework. That was the stan'ard after-school greetin'. The three of us satthere an' ate some warmed-up biscuits an' jam. We talked of pecan pies in the fall, an' the church picnic next week. Seemed there was always somethin' ta look forward ta.

Chapter 5

"Can Mr. Mel go?" I asked.

"Go where Honey?" Momma asked.

"Ta the church picnic," I said.

"I don't see why not? Everyone's invited."

I ran out the screen door lookin' fer Mel. I found him back at Pa's horseshoe pit, where Pa would throw shoes sometimes. As I got ta him, he turned ta me.

"You know, I've never played this game before."

"Pa could show you. He's real good, an' I'm not sayin' it 'cause he's my pa."

"Maybe I'll ask him ta give me a lesson after supper."

"Mr. Mel," I began. "Next Sunday, there's a church picnic after service. Everyone goes. Will you go with our family?"

"Will your Pa be there?"

"Pa always goes ta the picnic; he'll even go ta service."

"Well then, I think I can make it."

'This was goin' ta be grand.' I thought.

"Whatcha two doin'?" Pa asked as he approached. "I got some hens need feedin', Eula, an' Mel, if you can help me load the chicken wire inta the wagon, I can drop it off over at Joe's tomorrow."

"Sure, I'd be happy to."

"Pa, Mel doesn't know how ta pitch shoes. Could you give him a couple o' lessons before the picnic next Sunday?" I asked.

I knew that horseshoes was a weakness o' my pa's. Fer some men the bottle is mighty temptin', fer others it could be women or gamblin', but fer my pa it was pitchin' horseshoes. He was nicknamed 'one more game' Otis. He could throw good too! When he was outback you'd always hear the clangin' of metal on metal, the shoes hittin' the posts.

"I think Mel an' I could come out here after supper," Pa supposed.

"That would be fun, Otis," Mel agreed.

I was off ta the coop. Pa an' Mel started loadin' up the wagon. Pa an' Uncle Joe mostly bought everythin' together. If'n Uncle Joe needed some tack or truck, Pa would help pay an' they'd share it down ta the last nail. I never saw 'em fight or argue. They would tease each other but never fight.

"I'm takin' this wire ta Joe's place," Pa called out. "Tell your ma I'll be back in time fer supper."

"Need some help with that? "Mel asked. "No, I

can take care o' this. Thanks anyway."

Pa rolled the leather reins over the back of our horse, Blue Boy, an' headed ta Uncle Joe's. As I jumped up the back stairs, Momma came out on the stoop with a shirt in hand.

"Mel!" she called, "Child, where is Mr. Mel?"

Mel came 'round the corner o' the house. "Yes, Ma'am, what can I be doin' fer you?"

"You could try this on, an' let me see how it fits," Momma said as she handed the shirt ta Mel she was makin' out o' the fabric Mel had given her. Momma turned 'round as well as turnin' me 'round so's that Mel could have himself a little privacy out on our back porch. It fit him real well. Momma fussed with the collar an' the cuffs.

"I'll finish it up after supper."

"Thank you, Annie, it feels real good. I'll wear it ta Meetin' next Sunday. Is there gonna be any material left? Could you make a ban'ana fer Eula an' a handkerchief fer Billy?"

"Sure. Thank you, Mel, they'll like that."

"Did Eula tell you 'bout the picnic next Sunday?" Momma asked.

"Yes, she did. I'm plannin' on goin'."

"You'll have a good time. Don't you worry, I'll be fryin' up plenty o' chicken fer us ta take."

"Momma, Pa's goin' ta teach Mel how ta throw horseshoes after supper."

"You never played, Mel?" Momma asked.

"No... no, I haven't. I hear Otis will be a good teacher."

"Otis is good."

"See, Mel, I told you."

Momma an' I were cleanin' up the last of the dishes when I heard the first clang of a horseshoe hittin' its mark.

"Go on, Eula. You can go watch. Just 'member your Pa is givin' Mel a lesson, so you stay out o' the way." Her words were still in her mouth as I bounded down the stairs an' ran ta where they were. Little Bill was already there, sittin' on the grass watchin' the men play. I settled down next ta him.

"How's Mr. Mel doin'?" I asked.

"Pa's just now showin' him how ta toss that shoe."

"Mel, you're right-handed, so lead with your right foot. As you take that step, let your arm fall an' swing back. As you step ferward with your left foot, kinda plant your right foot on the ball an' toes, then swing your arm straight up an' give your right hip just a bit of a turn. That should give you the power so the shoe will have the distance you need."

"When should I let go?" Mel asked

"When it hits you in the head!" Billy laughed.

Mel smiled. Pa wasn't smilin' - not mad - just

not smilin'.

"I find it best ta release it 'bout three-quarters up. You need ta have a little height on the shoe so's it drops in an' hugs the ground. You don't want it comin' in flat an' skiddin' by the post or hittin' an' runnin' end over end like a chicken with its head cut off."

"No, I wouldn't want that," Mel confirmed.

Mel looked at us with a funny face, like he was 'bout ta jump off a high cliff inta a river of gators. We laughed.

"Could you show me one more time, Otis?" Mel asked. "You have such a constant movement."

"Sure."

Pa studied that post, holdin' the shoe with two hands, Pa swung it at its target. CLANG! The sound echoed 'round the house an' through the stand of woods.

"Good throw," Mel admired the shoe layin' sideways up against the post.

Pa was not so pleased.

"I didn't let it go early enough, an' I twisted my wrist at the last second. That's why the shoe turned instead of stayin' open. You want the mouth of the shoe open ta gobble up that post."

'Step, drop, plant, throw...it seems easy enough.' Mel thought out loud.

Now I'll never ferget how well Mel took ta instructions. I'll bet he was a good student. He tossed that shoe just the way Pa showed him. It landed 'bout eight feet short, but he looked so good.

"Mel, you should've eaten a little more supper. It might've given you the strength ta toss that shoe just a bit further. Look at this," Pa said as he an' Mel went ta pick up all the shoes.

"Your shoe landed open ta the stake. Now you just can't teach that. You had a good rotation on that shoe, an' a good form with that throw. As my brother, Joe, says, 'you got ta flow with the throw.' Here, throw these."

Pa dropped a half a dozen shoes by Mel an' stepped back. Mel threw those horseshoes, and each one landed closer than the last. CLANG rang out.

"That's a leaner!" I yelled when I saw the horseshoe propped up against the stake.

"You're doin' good, Mel, real good," Pa encouraged.

"You're not as good as my pa." Billy smiled at Pa, always keepin' on his good side.

Mel seemed ta be concentratin' real hard. Another shoe landed open just inches from the mark.

"You're throwin' 'em good!" Pa said. I could tell Pa was excited. He'd have someone ta play with after chores.

"Now go throw 'em back the other way, an' 'member always stand ta the right o' the post, an' don't go past it 'til you let go o' the shoe."

Pa put his hands on his hips an' smiled down at us as we sat on the grass. He looked as if he just built somethin' an' he was real proud of it.

"Eula, get us some tea, Darlin'. Billy, go git me a foldin' chair from the porch, bring a couple, an' tell your ma ta come out here awhile."

We ran at Pa's biddin'. We were back in a flash so we wouldn't miss anythin'. We sat with Momma an' Pa watchin' Mel throw those shoes. Pa was sippin' tea, Momma finishin' up Mel's shirt. Mel walked back an' forth over a dozen times. With each pass, he became more confidant an' deliberate with his toss.

"Well, you ready fer a game?" Pa asked.

"The question is do you think I am?" Mel raised his eyebrows at us.

"Okay, you're down there an' I'll start from here. The game is up ta twenty-one. A ringer is worth three points, an' a shoe in count, is worth 1 point."

"A shoe in count?" Mel questioned.

"A shoe landin' within a horseshoe width from the stake," Pa explained.

"The mouth of the shoe or the shoulders?" Mel continued.

"Do you want ta play or talk?" Billy bullied Mel.

"You hush boy. He doesn't know the game,"

Momma warned.

I put a cricket on his neck that I found crawlin' through the grass. He squiggled 'round gettin' it out o' his undershirt.

"Momma," he whined.

"Billy, settle down or go play somewhere else," Momma told him.

"Billy, is that bee sting still sore? It still looks red ta me," I dangerously asked.

"It's fine," he huffed as he turned an' set himself ta watch the game in silence.

Mel never stood a chance that spring evenin'. Pa gave Billy a lot ta cheer 'bout. Ringers, leaners, shoes landed a cat whisker away. Still, Mel threw pretty respectable, fer his first game, twenty-one ta eight.

"You practice this week, an' you might be able ta win a few matches at the picnic next Sunday," Pa said.

Mel had a hopeless smile as he picked up the shoes an' returned 'em ta the rail where Pa kept 'em.

"Come on, Mel, let's play one more," Pa insisted with a smile.

Momma was smilin', too.

"He always does that, an' when I want one more story at bedtime I never get it," Little Bill complained.

With that, Mel found his mark an' threw a ringer.

"How many points is that?" Mel asked like he didn't know.

Pa threw his shoe. CLANG.

" Same as that - three points, Mel."

Mel had a better game. He got eleven points before Pa took him ta task. They played five games that night. One game Mel only scored three points before Pa beat 'im.

"Otis, thank you fer soundly teachin' me a lesson in humility. Just when I thought I was goin' ta get a leg up on ya, you'd toss a ringer."

"Mel, I've been doin' this a long time. You keep at it, an' you'll be a pretty good player. You, too," Pa was pointin' at little Bill an' me. "Time fer bed."

"Say goodnight ta Mel, children, an' off ta bed," Momma supported.

"Good night, Mr. Mel," we chimed together an' off we went.

Momma handed Mel his shirt as we went ta bed. It was a blue cotton with a thin white stripe. He thanked her fer her time as he headed ta the shed. I looked back ta see Pa put his arm 'round Momma as they walked ta the house. I always felt good an' safe when they showed they were in love.

As we lay in bed that night, Momma told us a story. When she was done, she kissed our ferheads an' started ta leave the room.

"One more Momma, "little Bill begged. "Just one,

please, I can't go ta sleep, I'll lay here all night. PLEASE!!"

Momma smiled as she came back an' sat on the edge o' little Bill's feather bed. Maybe it was the "boy" she saw in Pa that night playin' one more game. Maybe it was a mother's soft heart; it didn't matter. I didn't hear the end of that story; I don't even 'member what it was 'bout. I do 'member my mother's willin'ness ta love on us a few more minutes that night.

"You see, boy," the old women shared, "you take the time, an' you give the time ta those you love. That's what they'll 'member when you're gone."

The boy looked at her and gently took her hand. "I remember a lot of bed time stories and a lot of milk and cookies after school."

"Do you 'member my fried chicken?"

"My friend's still call you "Fried-chicken Grandma."

"Are you hungry?" she asked. "Maybe you should go down ta the cafeteria."

"No, no I'm fine. I ate a little while ago. Do you need something?"

"I'm fine," she assured.

"Oh, where was I?" she asked, reachin' back ta memories long ago.

"Oh yes!"

That week went real good at school; no fightin'

71

with mean old boys an' Mel was gittin' a lot better at tossin' horseshoes. Pa had someone ta help git all the work done. Our farm never looked so good. Mel was organizin' thin's an' set up a burn pile an' cleaned out a lot old briers an' limbs Pa would never git ta. I'm sure Momma was happy ta see all Mel was doin'. Pa was able ta stay out in the fields; he never did boss Mel 'round. Mel seemed ta know what needed done, an' he did it. They spent a little time on that old stump every day. I think they liked beatin' it up together.

Chapter 6

That Saturday would be a day I thought 'bout a lot throughout my life, tryin' ta discern what was real, an' what were childish interpretations of things seen. That mornin' started off like most Saturdays. Billy an' I were out doin' our chores, waterin' an' feedin' hens an' hogs. We had just finished up an' Billy wanted ta go off lookin' fer rabbits an' squirrels. Pa called us ta the house.

"We're goin' ta market today. Change your clothes. We'll be leavin' as soon as I hitch up Blue Boy," he said.

"Honey, look what I got fer you. Mr. Mel had some leftover material from his shirt. He asked me ta make you this ban'dana fer your hair, an' this hankie fer Billy. You go an' thank him now," Momma instructed.

"Mr. Mel, Mr. Mel!" I called as I ran towards the barn.

He came out an' when he saw me, a smile slipped across his face. "Hey, who is this? Oh yeah. Eula?

Right? I didn't recognize you with that pretty blue bandana."

"Thank-you, Mr. Mel. Momma said you gave her this material fer me."

"Your welcome, Pumpkin. I hope you like it. You need ta thank your Ma. She's the one who made it."

"Are you goin' ta town with us, Mr. Mel?"

"Yes, I am!"

"I'm gonna help your pa hitch up the wagon right now."

"You ready, Eula?" Pa asked as he approached us.

"Yes, sir. Did you see my bandana? It matches Mr. Mel's shirt Momma made."

"It sure does. Looks real pretty. I won't have a hard time spyin' you in a crowd today."

Pa an' Mel hitched up the wagon an' little Bill an' I were soon loaded up in the back. The road Pa took ta town went past Janey an' Dorothy's farm. We always stopped both ways. Goin ta town an' vistin'! What a great day!"

As we approached their property, the girls came runnin' up ta the wagon.

Pa stopped the wagon. He didn't want ta roll over Janey's toes. She always tried ta hop on. Pa would never correct the girl. On the other hand, Uncle Joe had no problem tellin' me an' Billy how ta behave.

"Go on, get out. You got five minutes with your cousins, then we're off ta town," Pa said. He always told us we had five minutes. I later learned five minutes in adult time could mean one minute ta two hours!

"Good mornin', girls, " Momma said.

"Mornin', Aunt Annie. Mornin', Uncle Otis. Mornin', Mr. Mel," the girls issued all the proper greetin's, an' we were off.

I saw Aunt Lee greet Mel. She was a woman of tall stature, an' good humor. She had ta be, married ta Uncle Joe an' all. Aunt Lee was a woman among women. I watched her bake a pie, hammer a fence, an' hitch a team of horses. It seemed like there was nothin' she couldn't do, except handle raw meat. She couldn't gut it, clean it, or put it in a pan. My momma joked that's why she married Uncle Joe, so he could help her cook. We ran 'round the yard a bit then, over ta see the kittens that had been born that week. They had 'em in a box in the barn. When we got there, the adults were chatterin' 'bout this an' that.

"Mr. Mel, want ta see some kittens?" I asked as we passed by.

"Sure I would."

As we got in the barn with Mel on our heels, Dorothy stood by the box cryin'.

"What's the matter, child?" Mel asked.

"That little calico died," she sniffed.

"Oh, let's see."

Mel reached down an' lifted the limp little ferm from the box. He held it down fer all ta see as he stroked its belly with his fin'er. The kitten's nose twitched, its eyes popped open wide, an' so did Dorothy's. Then that kitten flipped itself 'round on his feet upright, right there in the palm of Mel's hand. A cheer went up, which caught the attention of the parents.

"It appears I woke up a sleepy head kitten," Mel said, explainin' the outburst. Mel placed the calico back in the back in the box, shoved his hands deep in his pockets, smiled an' rejoined the adults. Soon Pa had us back on the wagon an' headed fer town. We was ta pick up a thing or two fer Uncle Joe. As we came 'round a bend in the road there amidst the dense trees an' underbrush, drinkin' from Thornapple Creek was a pure white fawn. Pa stopped the wagon an' we just stared in total silence. He didn't move; he was watchin' us. His eyes were piercin'ly black an' stood out against it's white face; its tail an' ears stood straight up. We never saw a doe. The young deer slipped through the thick bush an' disappeared into the woods.

"That was the prettiest animal I've ever seen," Momma whispered, fearin' the deer might return only ta be scared off by her voice.

"She was beautiful," I awed.

"I'd like ta shoot her an' sell her hide fer one

hundred dollars!" Billy claimed.

Momma an' me turned an' looked at Billy tryin' ta figure out who exactly he belonged ta.

"An animal like that isn't fer meat, hides an' such. They're ta be enjoyed, an' ta be watched in wonder," Pa said as he tried ta teach Billy a lesson in the value of nature.

"The Dakota, Nakota, an' the Lakota Indians of the Sioux Nation believe when a white buffalo is born, it's of a great religious significance, a sign of peace, a unity among peoples, families an' nations. At least that's what I've heard," Mel said as he readjusted his place on the wagon bench next ta Momma.

"That weren't no buffalo. Mr. Mel, that was a deer," Billy pointed out.

"He was just tellin' us a fact, Little Bill, 'bout the white buffalo. It kinda came into his head upon seein' the white deer an' all. Right, Mr. Mel?" I told Billy, sayin' each word slow an' deliberate so he could understan' it through his thick skull.

"Maybe the deer is an omen of sorts?" Billy questioned.

"I don't know 'bout omens child, but I know when God shares a thin' of beauty, I just have to give Him thanks," Mel concluded.

Pa gave a giddy-up ta Blue Boy, an' we were off again. The grown-ups sat with their backs ta us in grown-up conversation. Billy was throwin' stones at trees an' fence posts, he had gathered 'em from Aunts Lee's yard. I was lyin' on my back bumpin' along watchin' the clouds pass by while protectin' my noggin from bangin' the wooden floorboards with each little jolt. I started thinkin' of that white deer an' if God did show us signs from time ta time. If miracles happened 'round us, an' we were just too busy, or too dumb ta see 'em. An' what 'bout that kitten, was it really sleep? I thought of that first day when I met Mel, he seemed ta come out of nowhere. I 'member the way my mind's eye pictured little Bill with the water washin' all 'round him. As I lay there thinkin' of all these thin's, I rolled my eyes up; an' looked at Pa, Momma an' Mel jostlin' ta an' fro in the front of the wagon. From my vantage point, they were upside down. Their heads an' bodies seemed ta be floatin' in the sky. Just then, Mel turned towards me an' gave me a wink an' a smile, like he was in my brain, readin' my thoughts. I quick sat up an' leaned against the wagon wall.

Abruptly Momma turned an' asked, "What is it, child?"

"There was a bee buzzin' 'round my head," I fibbed, not wantin' ta share my closest thoughts.

"Maybe it's the same one that got Billy down by the creek, " Mel said as he turned back facin' the road.

That Mel, maybe he was a mind reader. Maybe he had worked in a circus or a carnival as "The Great Mel", Seer, Soothsayer, an' Mystic Marvel of All That is Hidden. The more I thought, the more my imagination took over, an' the more I imagined, the more I was convinced that Mel just hadn't been walkin' through the woods that Friday afternoon. There was a powerful ferce movin' here in Thornapple County, an' only I was aware of its presence. That was a big responsibility. I couldn't tell Pa an' Momma. They would chalk it up ta the wild imagination of a child. Billy was just far too young, an' Mel, he was at the heart of the goin's on. I was gonna keep a close eye on his dealin's. As we got closer ta town, familiar faces an' families began ta pass us on the road. A hi here, an' a wave there an' my mind began ta slow down. I saw Faye an' Darwin Marsh. They went ta school with Billy an' me They were both older, but they were always kind.

"All right, you two, stay close ta your Ma. If she can't swat you, you're too far away," Pa instructed.

"Now, Otis, don't put 'em under my feet. Children, I need ta know where you are at all times," Momma reinstructed.

Pa tied up the wagon an' helped Momma down.

"Mel, you been in town here before?" Pa asked.

"No, I haven't," Mel said, as he looked 'round.

"The general store is across the street. The

owner's name is Marie. She's the one who knows everythin' there is ta know. Just let her in on you're stayin' out with us. Annie, I'm gonna check on that order I have at the mill."

"What'cha got ordered, Otis?" Mel inquired.

"Some lumber. I ordered it a couple weeks back. I want ta build the worktable fer the barn. I also got some fence posts. We got some needin' replacin.' I got ta get some odds an' ends fer repairs."

"You want me ta pick up a bucket of whitewash ta keep the weather off the wood, you buy fer repair?"

"No, Joe's got some; I'll pick it up on the way home."

Now Billy an' I loved walkin' 'round the store. They had everythin' a body could use. Blankets, food, tools, dresses, guns, dynamite, toys, books, an' if they didn't have it in the store, they could order anythin'. Once, the Browns ordered a washin' machine. We kept close ta Momma 'til somethin' caught this young girl's eye. In a case on a white linen cloth was a silver cross necklace. I could never bring myself ta ever ask fer such a gift. This cross had two smaller crosses on either side of the main one. I had never seen one like this before.

"Why do you think there's two crosses on each side of the middle one?" a voice asked from above.

I looked up ta see Mel standin' over me, lookin' at the object of my interest.

"I'm not sure, but it's still pretty."

"It could be those two crosses represent the two thieves who hung on either side of Jesus when he was crucified."

"Maybe," I responded, never lookin' up, thinkin' how wonderful it would ta be ta wear that cross ta church some Sunday mornin'.

Mel walked away, leavin' me ta my dreams. Billy kept close ta Momma as she stocked up on the staples we needed. Mel walked up toMiss Marie as she stood behind the counter.

"Can I help you, sir?" she asked.

"Yes, Ma'am, I could use a pair of work shoes, an' three pairs of socks. I'd also like a bit of that rock can'y."

"What size shoe do you wear?" she asked.

"Size ten."

"Would you like brown or black?"

"Brown would be fine. Could I get an extra pair of laces?"

"You surely may."

Billy's ears perked up as high as mine when we heard Mel order up rock can'y. We watched as Miss Marie took out pieces of stones made from sugar.

"Oh, put a few more in there," Mel said, as he supervised the purchase.

"That'll be three dollars an' sixty-eight cents," Marie added.

Mel reached inta his pocket an' pulled out a small leather pouch. He loosened the drawstrin', reachin' in with his thumb an' ferefin'er removin' a shiny new ten-dollar gold piece.

"Well, I don't see these very often; looks brand new! You can still see all the feathers on the headdress. Usually, they're all worn down."

"I just made that one this mornin'," Mel joked with a smile.

Miss Marie counted out Mel's change an' handed him his package. Mel nodded an' headed out the door. Momma finished her order. Everythin' would remain there 'til Pa would come back an' pay. When we stepped out of the store, we saw Pa comin' towards us from the mill; Mel was nowhere ta be seen.

'Now, where did he go?' I thought, concerned 'bout the safety of the rock can'y. The town was small, but it was the world ta little Bill an' me. There was the general store, the livery that sold feed an' tack, two doctor's offices, one fer people, one fer animals. There was a lumber mill at one end of town. There was a boardin' house that served food ta the public, an' one saloon. There was a bank where Mr. Roy worked, a plumbin' business an' a dentist's office that the An'erson brothers ran. Billy was there once. He squealed like a stuck pig fer hours. That was our world, seemed pretty big comin' from the farm. Town was always movin' fast. People walkin' in an' out of stores an' businesses, people talkin' on the street. Seemed pretty excitin'.

"You done?" Pa called out ta Momma.

"Yes I am."

"I'll load this up, an' I thought we'd get a piece of pie at Mildred's," he replied, referrin' ta the boardin' house.

"We'll meet you there. I want ta stop at Doctor Wilson's. I need ta get some medicine; I'm out."

Momma always had hard "woman days," as she'd explain. Doc Wilson made a fortune on an elixir called "Eve's Solution." Women wanted it cause, well, it relieved some pain. Men wanted it cause it relieved some pain fer 'em, too. I tasted it once. It was a strong bitter taste, an' if you took enough of it, it'd make you dizzy. I never enjoyed dizziness. After gettin' Momma's prescription filled, we headed across the street ta Mildred's. As we crossed the street, all three of us jumped at the sound of barkin' an' snappin' that exploded ta our right. Momma quick put her arm out 'round us an' placed herself between the sound an' us. It was Mr. Moyer. He seemed ta be an unpleasant man of low moral character an' ignorance of the benefits of cleanliness. His only companions were the dogs he kept. Every child in Thornapple County would walk a mile out of his way ta avoid an encounter with 'em. It was told in schoolyard circles, Mr. Moyer would feed his dogs on the flesh o' children who'd gone missin'. I never knew of any missin' children, but we were certain they was ta be eaten if'n they did. The dogs strained at their tethers. Mr. Moyer seemed ta keep 'em just barely out of reach. Their teeth were bared an' white. Their barkin' attracted the concerned eyes of all within earshot.

"Git down! Git down, I said," Mr. Moyer barked at the dogs.

As I stood there with Momma an' Billy, I prayed that those tethers would hold. Then seemin'ly out of nowhere, Mel walked up between us, an' the hounds of Hades.

"Whoa, they're a bit wound up today, aren't they?"

"Don't you be worryin' 'bout my animals!" Mr. Moyer shot back.

"I'm not. They're fine dogs. I bet they hunt good!" Mel complimented.

Mr. Moyer was taken back by Mel's friendly manner. I watched as Mel kinda brought up his right hand ta his waist in a very unnoticeable movement. Exposin' his palm in the direction of the dogs. At once, they seemed ta calm down. No longer did they jump an' strain at their tethers. Mel continued ta talk ta Mr. Moyer askin' him one question an' then another 'bout his dogs. Mr. Moyer seemed ta enjoy this stranger takin' an interest his pets. I saw as Mel lowered his hand, all three dogs laid down in the dusty street. Momma, Billy, an' I just stood there.

"You been breedin' these animals fer awhile, you say?" Mel asked.

"Years," Mr. Moyer confirmed.

Mel went down ta one knee an' called the dogs ta him. Mr. Moyer reacted sharply by double wrappin' the tether 'round his hand. He was too slow; the dogs were on Mel like a tick. They rubbed up against him an' licked his face an' hands. He tried ta move his head this way an' that, but those hounds still gave him a bath. Momma was even taken back that Mel wasn't bein' served up as lunch.

"You must really know dogs," Mr. Moyer said in disbelief. "My dogs never cotton to any one but me!"

"Dogs are a reflection of their master, their trainer. If they're loved they will show that," Mel observed.

"I do love 'em."

"I love dogs," Little Bill's small voice interrupted the flow of conversation.

"Well, say there, boy. My Sally's due with a litter of pups next week. You ask your Ma an' Pa, an' if they let you, you can come get one after she weans 'em," Mr. Moyer offered.

Givin' away a puppy? Who is this man? I never

talked ta him before or even seen anyone talk ta him, or as a matter of fact, I NEVER heard of anyone ever talkin' ta him before. An' now he's offerin' Billy, a puppy.

Pa walked up ta this gatherin' of sorts. "Everythin' okay?" he questioned.

"Mr. Moyer's gonna give me a puppy if you say it's okay, Pa."

Pa could have been knocked down with a feather. He looked 'round ta see what he had missed.

"That's nice, son," Pa said, searchin' fer the piece of the puzzle that would help make sense of this conversation.

"I'll explain it over pie, Otis," Momma said. "Thank you, Mr. Moyer. You let us know 'bout that pup."

Momma got us all movin' in the direction of Mildred's. Mel remained in conversation with Mr. Moyer.

"What's goin' on?" Pa asked once we crossed the street.

"I'm not sure," Momma started. "Those dogs came up on us like we had just taken their last bone. Then Mel came up, an' the dogs an' Mr. Moyer took ta him. I've never seen anyone pet those animals before," Momma remembered.

"Never saw Mr. Moyer with what resembled a smile before," Pa stated, Billy an' I laughed.

"Hush you two. Otis, don't make fun of the man in front of the children."

"Annie, I'm not makin' fun, I just don't remem…"

"Otis!" Momma stopped him in mid-sentence.

Mel was still talkin ta Mr. Moyer as we went fer our slices of pie, a rare treat. Pa an' Momma got coffee; we got milk. Mel soon joined us. Miss Mildred's boardin' house was the biggest house 'round. When you walked in, there was a pretty mahogany staircase, which swirled 'round ta a second story landin'. It had an ornate chandelier with faceted crystal glass bobbles. As you stood facin' the staircase, ta the left was a sittin' room where the people who lived there could be social. It was filled with paintin's, divans an' high back chairs. Ta the right was where we would dine, a room that could hold a Gilbert family reunion. There was one long special table fer those who lived there; an' smaller tables fer the public trade. I 'member the floral embossed wallpaper, an' the rich tapestry-like drapes. It was a grand place.

"What kinda pie do we have today?" Pa asked the young girl waitin' on us.

"We have pecan, apple an' a few slices of peach," she replied.

"We'll all have pecan, Pa ordered. "Mel, how 'bout you?"

"Make mine pecan, too," Mel said.

The girl went back ta fill our order. Pa took a breath, looked at Mel an' Momma.

"What in the name of thunder was goin' on out there?"

"I'm gettin' a puppy!" Little Bill stated lest anyone ferget.

"I'm talkin' ta the adults, Billy." Pa said, turnin' an' lookin' ta Momma an' Mel.

Momma was still befuddled as ta what happened. Mel was more surprised at Pa's amazement.

"Well," Mel begun, "I saw Annie an' the children talkin' ta that Mr. Moyer."

"We were bein' set upon by his dogs; I dared not move. I thought the children an' I would be attacked," Momma broke in.

"You were scared? I thought you knew him? That's why I came over, I just wanted ta meet him."

"I'm gonna get my puppy, aren't I?" Billy reminded everyone of his main interest.

"I thought you were protectin' us," Momma said ta Mel. "I was sure those dogs were fixin' ta tear us apart."

Momma was still a little shaken. I know she was afraid fer little Billy an' me. Pa was still tryin' ta figure out why he wasn't outside with an axe handle beatin' those dogs ta death, an' maybe givin' Mr. Moyer a whack or two.

88

"If you hadn't come along, Mel . . . I don't know what would've happened."

Pa put his hand on Momma's. "Thank you, Mel fer comin' along when you did," Pa said

"I really didn't' do anythin'," Mel protested. "I just talked ta the man an' petted his dogs. I did ask him if he ever went to church. I told him y'all have a good meetin' every Sunday an' I invited to the church picnic. I told him he should leave the dogs at home. There'd be a lot of people there an' it might make 'em nervous."

Pa an' Momma just sat there. I don't think anyone would have ever thought ta invite Mr. Moyer ta anythin'.

"He seems like a nice fellow, an' he's heard what a good cook you are, Annie. He said next time he slaughters a head of beef; he'd be willin' ta trade some choice meat fer your home cookin' an' baked goods."

Mel had made a friend everyone else had either overlooked or shunned. It seemed he brought us inta the deal as well. Right now, I'm sure that was gonna be okay, 'cause Pa loved beefsteaks, an' Billy wanted a dog.

"I hope I wasn't too forward. He seemed like a nice man, a bit lonely, but a nice man."

"No, that's okay. I'd be happy cookin' a bit extra in trade fer some beef," Momma said. "I'm just surprised. This mornin', I had never spoke ta the man an' now I'll be cookin' fer him."

"An' he'll be givin' me a puppy!" Billy proclaimed with a big smile.

"Yes, Billy," Pa reaffirmed. "You'll be gettin'' a puppy."

With that, our pastries came, an' we honored those pies with the silence they deserved. There were a few well-placed moans of enjoyment. There was also the traditional smackin' of the lips, but the topic of Mr. Moyer was laid ta rest, basically 'cause no one could understan' what had really happened in those few moments. Pa paid fer the treat. Mel wanted ta chip in, but Pa wouldn't hear of it. Mel offered ta take the wagon ta the mill ta be loaded up. Pa wanted ta get some tobacco before we left town. From time to time, Pa would roll his own cigarettes, out of the sight of wives an' young'uns. Mel brought the loaded wagon 'round an' we started on the journey home. As we neared the creek where we spotted the white fawn, our eyes strained as we peered through the trees an' underbrush, hopin' just ta catch one last glimpse of it. I would only see it one other time in my life. No matter, I always looked fer it whenever I passed that spot.

Chapter 7

We stopped at Uncle Joe's place on the way home. We told the girls 'bout Mr. Moyer an' his dogs. They couldn't believe we were still alive! They were jealous we ate at Mildred's, Uncle Joe didn't believe in eatin' out. None of 'em had heard tell of a white fawn bein' spotted 'round these parts. Uncle Joe thought he an' Billy should go huntin'. Momma said she knew where Billy got it from. Momma dropped some thin's ta Aunt Lee; Pa picked up some whitewash. Momma started tellin' Aunt Lee an' Uncle Joe 'bout Mr. Moyer. They stood there shocked.

"You know, Johnny would talk ta that Darryl Moyer from time ta time. You should ask him what Darryl's story is." Uncle Joe said. "He an' Johnny are the same age." Uncle Johnny was Pa's oldest brother, the one who got off the farm.

"Mel reachin' in the mouth of a catfish is one thin', but those dogs, all you gonna brin' back is a bloody stump." Uncle Joe cautioned. Mel kinda sloughed it off, like Momma was makin' more ta it than there was.

I thought a lot 'bout that day as my head lay on the pillow that night. The white fawn, Mr. Moyer, his dogs an' how Mel seemed ta control 'em. Even that gold coin. Where did he get it? How come it was so new? It seemed odd ta Miss Marie like maybe Mel had robbed a city bank an' he come here ta spend his loot. An' what 'bout in the wagon, I swear he was readin' my mind! As my mind relaxed, my thoughts turned from today ta the morrow. The church picnic, all the kids' playin' together, tables of food, games; it would be a good time. Maybe Mel might speak ta Miss Flo or the widow Hawkins. Who knows what the morrow would bring. I laid in the quiet of the night. Only the sound of little Bill's breathin', an' a few crickets rippled the silence. I fell asleep prayin', prayin' fer my family an' the things I thought I saw. I prayed fer weather, the picnic, crops, friends, things a child finds important. I thanked God fer the trip ta town, an' I found myself prayin' fer Mr. Moyer. Imagine that! What kinda world are we livin' in when children start prayin' fer the Mr. Moyer's? I figured it must be a better one than the day before.

"Good night, Honey," Momma said from the doorway.

"Good night," I returned. "Love ya."

"I love you, too. Get a good night's rest. We've

got a big day tomorrow. You'll be needin' all your strength if your gonna win some races!"

I fell asleep, a good sleep. The kinda sleep a child enjoys, restful an' safe, knowin' you're protected an' loved. The sounds of the house are familiar an' of comfort. The sounds from outside cause you no fear 'cause your parents sleep between them an' you. You find your sweet spot in the mattress, an' the covers lay on you heavy like a coat of armor. I 'member that feelin', that was the home I was raised in. That's the testament ta my parents. Billy was up earlier than usual as if that would make the picnic come quicker. He wanted ta wear his play clothes ta church on account of the picnic afterwards. Momma was explainin' how he could change after church, 'cause play clothes aren't respectful in God's house. That's when Billy says the whole world's God's house, so maybe he should wear his church clothes all the time, kinda sassy. Pa walks by an' cracks him on the behind, a real good one. It took his breath away, more from surprise than pain. I checked out the window a couple of times ta see if Mel was up. I put on my dress an' heard his footsteps on the porch. The screen door's spring stretched as he opened it. The fresh coffee smell hung in the air. Breakfast was bein' served.

"Come on, you two, breakfast's gettin' cold," Momma called.

"Billy, hurry up," I prompted, more ta agitate than ta encourage.

"You just hold on, Eula. You're not the boss o' me," Billy snarled as he fastened his pants. "Comin', Momma!" he called.

"Bring down some clothes ta change inta after church," Momma reminded.

Sunday breakfast was biscuits, bacon, eggs, grits, an' gravy. That would hold us 'til the picnic. I looked over at Pa. He was dressed in his good pants an' shirt. He was goin' ta Meetin'! I liked it when he did; it made me feel like God was smilin' at us. Pa an' Mel went out an' hitched up Blue Boy. Momma an' I packed up the basket of food. We had chicken, pickles, corn bread, an' beans ta pass.

"Little Bill, bring me the good napkins," Momma requested. They were the ones Gran'ma Ada had embroidered; we used 'em on special occasions. Gran'ma Ada was my Mother's mother. She died when Momma was young. I could tell Momma missed her a lot. I knew there were times when Momma would've just liked ta sit down an' talk ta her.

"Come, children, we need ta git goin'! Your pa's waitin'. We want ta be on time," Momma hurried us along. Pa hated ta be late. We had an uneventful ride ta church, no signs from God drinkin' from the creek. When we arrived, Momma took our basket over to where the food was bein' keep. We headed in ta the service as a family, plus Mel. When we started ta take our regular pew, who was sittin' in front of us but Mr. Moyer! He was dressed an' bathed. He had on new but out-of-date clothes. His hair was slicked back. He smiled an' shook hands with Mel an' Pa. He looked a bit out of place, but I think he was real happy ta be there. His back was ta us most of the time, but I could see his smile. Billy stood behind Mr. Moyer an' tapped his shoulder.

"Good mornin', Mr. Moyer," Billy sung out. "How's your dog, Sally?"

"Good mornin', boy," Mr. Moyer replied, happy ta see another familiar face. "She's doin good. Any day now. If you ever want ta come over an' see her, you an' your Pa just stop by."

"How many pups does she usually have?" Billy asked.

"'Tween four an' six" was the answer.

"Boy, leave Mr. Moyer alone. Service is fixin' ta begin," Pa whispered.

"Sit with us at the picnic," Mel whispered a quick invite. "We have plenty."

Mel shot a wink an' a smile ta Momma. She returned it with a reassurin' smile an' nod. She had indeed considered Mr. Moyer's place at our table. Pa leant over ta Mr. Moyer.

"We'd be please ta have you sit with us."

Pa sat in the pew all stiff an' ridged; he looked out of place. Mel was at home in the pew, happy ta be there in a worshipful way. I was just glad my pa was there. I hoped he'd get a few tips from Mel. When we stood fer the first hymn, Mel handed a hymnal ta Mr. Moyer, turned ta the correct page number. I thought that was a friendly thin' ta do. I didn't pay much attention ta the service, other than Mr. Moyer sin'in' so loud an' so off-key. My mind was on the picnic followin' the meetin'. I saw Jane an' Dorothy. Across the sanctuary, I spied Betty, Hazel, an' Emily between adult shoulders. Betty saw me back. We both lit up with excitement. The final hymn was five verses! It took ferever. Everyone 'round us just listened ta Mr. Moyer lift his voice ta the Lord.

"You two will need ta go inta the choir room an' change," Momma instructed. "We'll meet you out front."

The adults all shuffled out, exchangin' niceties. Mr. Moyer was shakin' everybody's hand. I saw Mel speakin' ta Miss Melba; this could prove ta be a most interestin' day.

"Hurry up an' change," Janey said, stan'in' in the middle of the floor.

"There's a girl's side fer changin' an' a boy's side. Which side are you on?" Dorothy asked of her sister.

"I'm on the side of I don't care; I just want ta git goin'."

Soon we were walkin' through the ferest of adults in search of our parents. I spotted little Bill thru the men movin' tables; he was standin' next ta Momma. All the women were busy puttin' out dishes an' platters of food. The mother's were gatherin' up their brood like a hen with chicks.

"Eula Mae, you an' Billy get this table set before you take off. Set a place fer Mr. Moyer over there next ta Mel."

I looked 'round, takin' in the day. There were men settin' up tables; there was a group settin' up some horseshoe pits. Others had set up a big tent so some of the older folks could get out of the afternoon sun. The women were settin' tables, puttin' finishin' touches on dishes. There was a group of men an' women that were soakin' catfish fillets in milk gettin 'em ready ta deep fry up. The smells mingled with the sounds of preparation. Billy an' I finished our job an' we were off ta join our friends. They all had congregated by the pits. Uncle Joe, Mr. Homer, Mr. Roy. All of 'em were there.

"My Pa is the best horseshoe pitcher in the county," Little Bill announced.

"He is, is he?" Uncle Joe questioned as he scooped little Bill up an' over his shoulder, fer a playful swat on the britches.

"Hey," called Pa. "Don't whip him unless you mean it!" Pa had just finished pounded in a stake.

"Is it okay ta give him a blisterin'? "Uncle Joe joked. "I'm pretty good at it."

"Nobody's whippin' on me!" Billy yelled as he an' his buddies ran off fer the creek.

"So, Otis, who's your partner today?" Uncle Joe asked.

"Mel an' I are gonna take you all on. He's been pitchin' fer a week, an' I'd stack him up against all you knuckleheads."

"Knuckleheads! We'll show you who's a knucklehead, Otis Gilbert," Mr. Roy shouted. A chuckle went up from the group.

"Reverend, now no extra help this year," Uncle Joe said as the preacher came ta the pits.

"Is this the right distance?" the reverend asked.

"I measured it off twice," Pa assured.

"Well, I must be feelin' a bit strong today," the preacher flexed.

"Oh Lord, give me...." the reverend started.

"Hey, stop that!" Pa interrupted. "No outside help!"

"I don't know," Mel piped up. "You may need to get on your knees a few times yourself, Otis, if I'm your partner!"

A dozen or so men started ta gather at the horseshoe pits. Their jawin' back an' forth seemed almost as important as the game.

"Why, Otis," a voice in the back of the crowd

lofted ta the heavens.

"Haven't seen you at church since last year 'bout this time." It was Mr. Brinson.

"Well, Hank, I'm afraid every time you see me, it drudges up bad memories, seein' how bad I beat you last year. So you might say when I'm not at church, well, I'm bein' considerate of your feelin's an' all."

Mr. Brinson shook Pa's hand. "Good ta see you, Otis."

"It's a good day ta be seen. Have you met Mel?"

"No, I haven't. Hank Brinson," Mr. Brinson offered his hand ta Mel.

"Nice ta met you, an' this is Mr. Moyer," Mel introduced Mr. Moyer, who'd been standin' ta the side watchin' the men banter.

"Mr. Moyer, you look familiar. Are you from 'round these parts?" Mr. Brinson asked slyly.

"Hank, it's me, Darryl. I lived here all my life."

"Darryl, ... I'll be... boy, you clean up good! Welcome ta the picnic!"

"Darryl an' I grew up across the road from each other," Mr. Brinson addressed the men listenin'. "I didn't recognize you without your dogs! Darryl is the finest trainer of huntin' animals there is."

Mr. Brinson put his arm 'round Mr. Moyer.

"Darryl is my partner today," Mr. Brinson declared. "It'll be like old times. Who got you out here ta this picnic today?"

"It was Mel an' Otis there," Mr. Moyer replied.

This was a strange day. Seemed like Mr. Moyer had some old friends at church. Mel had a grin on his face a mile wide. He seemed ta take great satisfaction in Mr. Moyer bein' at church, an' the picnic, an' havin' a good time.

"Okay," the preacher started. "You need ta gather up in your families fer prayer before this meal."

We all moved towards our tables an' blankets. Jane an' Dorothy went with Uncle Joe.

"The board is spread. Let's give thanks."

The reverend prayed the food was blessed, an' the lines began. I was goin' ta git Miss Robert's sweet potatoes before they were gone. The plates an' bowls crowded each other on the tables. The colors an' variety tickled the senses. There was enough food ta feed an army. Mel got in line behind me. The rest of the Gilberts followed suit.

"What do you suggest?" Mel asked, lookin' fer some advice.

"You need ta try Miss Robert's sweet potatoes an' Aunt Lee's potato salad," I recommended. "Stay away from Mrs. Mertz's rice. She never cooks it long enough. I hate crunchy rice. Momma's fried chicken is the best; Mrs. Kin' 's is good too. Mrs. Strum's black-eyed peas has big hulks of ham. They butcher hogs fer a livin'. You gotta try Mrs. Jones rice puddin'! It's the creamiest."

I gave him as much infermation as I thought he could process. He was on his own now. I eyed the contents of each dish an' bowl before me. There's etiquette at a potluck. You must sample many dishes, but never too much of any one in peticuler, unless it's your Mom's. You can't take more meat than vegetables. You can't get more than two varieties of any kinda vegetable. Above all other rules, never take the last of anythin'. I got half way through the table, an' I ran out of room on my plate. I don't like thin's touchin' each other, so I reluctantly had ta retreat ta our table. The sun was smilin' on our picnic, an' a fly was buzzin' 'round my plate in a most irritatin' way. Billy sat down beside me, havin' disregarded all the rules of potluck. He began without a word ta scale the mountains of food he had heaped on his plate.

"You'll finish every bite," Pa warned.

"Billy, you'll never finish all that. It'll be wasted," Momma said sadly, askin' herself why she was standin' next ta him in line.

"He'll finish it alright," Pa's warnin' had turned inta a declaration.

"I'll finish, I'm starvin'!" Billy protested in between gulps.

"These sweet potatoes are good," Mel confirmed

"Wait till you try that puddin'; you'll thank me!"

Janey an' Dorothy came an' sat down at the table

with us, as did Mr. Moyer. There was kid talk an' adult talk, an' I had an ear in both conversations. Uncle Joe came over an' shooed Momma over ta his table where the women began ta mass. The men talked horseshoes, an' the children talked games. Billy cleaned his plate an' went back ta the tables ta see what he had missed. I lingered over my rice puddin', an' sample of peach cobble, courtesy of the preacher's wife.

"Do you think we'll play the same games as last year?" Dorothy asked. "'Cause I'm taller than I was last year, an' I won't slow anyone down in the three-legged race," She said, fishin' fer a partner.

"I'll have ta protect my title in the sack race," Janey said, remindin' us of her athletic abilities.

The men went ta pick over the tables, an' ta grab an extra win' or thigh. The women's table grew in size an' sound. The children were ready fer the contests ta begin.

"Gather 'round, children. The festivities are fixin' ta begin!" called Reverend Blanchard in a deep official voice.

"Get partnered up fer the three-legged race!"

Dorothy stood there lookin' fer someone ta make eye contact with.

"Over here, Dorothy," I called out. "I've got a piece of rope."

Dorothy ran ta me quick as a bunny. Then she

knelt down an' began ta cinch up the rope without a word.

"I'm ready."

As she put her arm 'round me, I secured mine 'round her waist. Pastor Blanchard looked over the participants, visually checkin' each lashin'. Once satisfied, he commanded us.

"Take your marks, get set, GO!" He shouted ta the heavens.

The course was lined with cheerin' parents. Sally Kruger an' her brother Paul fell with their first steps.

"Keep an eye on that big pecan tree!" Dorothy yelled. Then she started markin' our steps, an' holdin' me close.

"One, two, one, two," she counted. She quickened her count, an' we quickened our pace. Her lower jaw was set, the breeze in her hair. Her eyes were fixed on the finish line. I felt her determination as she pulled me tight under her arm.

"One, two, one, two." she continued ta count.

We broke inta a run. I felt like we were flyin'. Our stride was perfectly timed as we passed the finish line. The cheers an' applause from our parents rolled over the meadow. We were able ta keep our balance as we slowed down. Turnin' back, we saw that we had far an' away beaten our nearest competition. Dorothy started jumpin' up an' down, her arms wavin' overhead with excitement, causin' me ta fall an' her ta topple on top of me.

"I told you I had grown! I told you we could win!" she hollered.

I had had no expectations fer that race; I was just there ta be a good cousin, a good friend. Dorothy had lifted us ta victory. As we stood there, Pastor Blanchard presented us each with a decorated ribbon fer comin' in first place. I later found out that Dorothy had admired Janey's ribbon from the year before so much she had sworn she would win one this year! An' she did. I competed in the wheel barrel race with Billy 'cause I thought he was fast an' small. We finished in the middle of the pack. There was an egg throwin' contest, which Hazel an' I were out early; on accounta, she dropped the egg. Other races were ta begin, but with a ribbon pinned ta my blouse, my attention was turned ta the horseshoe pits. The familiar clang of the shoes strikin' the stakes drew me ta where the men were practicin'. There was Pa an' Mel stan'in' amongst the others waitin' fer their turn ta warm up. I liked seein' Pa out at the church picnic. He seemed so friendly, an' people liked him. Why, I bet if he was ta come ta church regular like, they'd ask him ta be a deacon! Then he could serve communion an' take up the offerin'. He wouldn't git ta sit with us 'cause he'd be at the back of the church with the other deacons, but he'd be at church, an' we could walk home together every week. Pa an' Mel took their places an' begin ta toss the shoes. Their distance was good; an' Pa was givin' Mel some last-minute pointers. As they stepped off ta the side ta wait fer their turn, Momma come up from behind an' put her hands on my shoulders.

"Have they started yet?" she asked.

"No, they're still practicin'," I replied.

"I saw you an' Dorothy win that three-legged race. You girls ran like the wind."

"Dorothy just took a hold of me, an' off we went!"

Aunt Lee approached our conversation catchin' the tail end.

"That girl was bound an' determined ta win that race today! How was the ride, Eula?"

"It was pretty fast, Ma'am."

"The men are goin' ta start throwin' shoes here in a minute; we'll need ta cheer 'em on," Momma told Aunt Lee.

"When is everybody goin' ta cheer on the wives who cooked all this food?" Aunt Lee playfully asked anyone in earshot. A weak cheer went up from the surroundin' chairs an' blankets as well as a few lifted drumsticks.

"Well that was more that last year!" she said as she settled back into her chair.

Momma spread out a blanket fer us, children, ta sit on. I was goin' ta cheer on Pa an' Mel. I'd cheer fer Uncle Joe an' Mr. Moyer when they weren't playin' against my pa. It was mid-afternoon an' the constant thuds an' clangs filled the meadow next ta the church. Little Bill an' the boys spent half the time down by the creek chasin' frogs an' turtles, an' the other half on our blanket. Pa an' Mel won their first match. Mel didn't help Pa out a lot, but more important, he didn't hurt him.

"Twenty-one ta twelve," Pa said as he came over an' sat on the blanket a moment. "Not bad, but we'll have ta do better if we hope ta make a showin'." Pa taok a sip from Momma's lemonade.

"I think I was releasin' the shoe just a hair early," Mel contemplated.

"You're doin just fine, Mel." Mel gave me a wink.

"I think you two will win it all," I said.

"Your Uncle Joe will have somethin' ta say 'bout that. He says he's winnin' the title this year," Aunt Lee informed us.

"You tell my baby brother when he grows up we'll let him play with the big boys," Pa instructed.

There were a half a dozen matches goin' on, an' I know my Pa knew the score of each one. He was sizin' up all the competitors.

"That Mr. Brinson is a good pitcher, he teamed up with Mr. Moyer. Now Darryl's a bit rusty, but you can tell he's thrown some shoes in his day. They're the ones we'll have ta watch out fer."

The games whittled down as the afternoon

slipped by. Uncle Joe an' his partner, Mr. Homer, lost a match ta Mr. Roy an' his son, Jeb. Mr. Roy really gave Uncle Joe the business. The sounds of the game fell into silence with the endin' of the matches. Pa an' Mel would face Mr. Brinson an' Mr. Moyer fer all the marbles. Mr. Moyer had a grin as wide as the Mississippi. It felt good that he was there an' havin' a good time an' not just some sad man sittin' in his house all alone. Pa an' Mel came over ta git some water before the game while the pits were bein' raked out.

"Mel, you're doin' real good. If I hadn't taught you last week, I'd swear you been playin' a long while," Pa said.

"Otis, how is your back?" Mel asked, seemin'ly out of concern.

"Fine. Why?" Pa asked.

"'Cause you've been carryin' this team from the first pitch!" Mel teased.

Momma laughed, so did I. Pa was right though; Mel was doin' a good job. Sometimes that happens. Everyone workin' together fer some common good, an' y'all draw from each other's strengths an' pretty soon people are doin' at a level they've never been before. Mr. Brinson stood near the pit clangin' two shoes together callin' Pa an' Mel ta the match. "Come on, boys, your lesson is fixin' ta begin."

Pa smiled an' showed the way ta Mel. A popcorn

of cheers rose up from the crowd, who were settlin' down ta watch the final match. As the men squared off, they shook hands. I heard Mr. Moyer tell Mel he was havin' a great time. It was one final game; winner take all. I thought how funny it would be if Pastor Blanchard would have ribbons ta pass out ta the winners. The sight of grown-ups sportin' ribbons pinned ta their chests!

"I often wondered in later years why I never heard horseshoe matches called on the radio or television. As a child, I found 'em pretty excitin'. It just seemed there was never much of an understandin' of the game." The old woman remarked to the "boy".

Little Bill an' a few of his friends marked their territory on the blanket as they watched the final match. Billy had one eye on the game an' the other on the frog he caught. Uncle Joe took a seat next ta Aunt Lee after pickin' over the table of sweets.

"Now you 'member everythin' I ever taught you, an' you might have a chance!" Uncle Joe called out ta Pa. Aunt Lee playfully slapped at his arm.

"Joe T, you are so bad! Just leave Otis alone."

The T stood fer Tommy, not Thomas. Mr. Brinson an' Mr. Moyer jumped out ta an early lead. They led the entire game by two ta three points. Pa made two ringers, but that Mr. Brinson was a real good pitcher. As Mr. Brinson took aim on the final pitch, the people crowded in on one another fer a good view. No one was walkin' away lookin' fer a chicken leg or a piece o' pie. Mr. Brinson stood with his feet together, studyin' his target. His hand drew back as he stepped into his pitch. He released the shoe with a 'umph' an' it sailed high. Mr. Brinson's shoe opened up perfect as it arched toward the post. It hooked dead center an' clanged 'round the stake, settlin' ta the ground. A cheer went up, an' Billy groaned! Winnin' that match made Mr. Moyer the happiest person at the picnic, next ta Dorothy. There was handshakes an' backslappin' all 'round. Pa an' Mel found a couple of empty chairs an' brought 'em over by us.

"We could never git out in front 'em. They just stayed a couple points in front of us," Pa said as he melted inta his seat.

"That Darryl sure did well. I heard he hasn't tossed a shoe-in twenty years," Mel added.

"Well, I heard tell someone out there had only been playin' 'bout a week!" Uncle Joe was spreadin' some gossip 'bout Mel he had picked up 'round the horseshoe pits.

"You did a fine job," he added.

"You were a good partner. Wish I could have brought us home," Pa regretted.

"I'm glad Mr. Moyer had such a good time," Momma said.

"I can hardly believe he was here. After all those

years of cuttin' him an' his dogs a wide berth, he shows up all smiles an' grins," Aunt Lee leaned ferward an' whispered.

"Well, he doesn't live but a piece down the road from either of you," Mel said out loud.

"We ain't exactly neighbors," Uncle Joe excused.

"Who are your neighbors?" Mel asked.

"Who do you think my neighbors should be?" Uncle Joe asked, wonderin' where this all was goin'.

Pa sat silently as Uncle Joe was 'bout ta learn who his neighbor was.

"Back east, there was a salesman broke down on the side of the road. He was carryin' books an' cutlery 'round ta homes an' farms outside of towns. It seemed his axel pin busted an' the wheel come off. He couldn't get the pin out of the hole, an' he didn't have another once he did. Well, along comes this fellow. He happened ta be the mayor of a small town in the next county over. He saw the man needed help, but he was on his way ta an important meetin'. He told the man he couldn't help an' continued down the road.

"Politicians are 'bout as useful as a bucket of water in a rain storm," Uncle Joe said.

It got a smirk from Pa. Mel went on, not mindin' the comment.

"Then the man saw another wagon comin' down the road. It happened ta be a deacon from the local church. He was headed ta town with some fresh milk. He barely explained he couldn't chance the milk spoilin' as he rolled on by.

"Then the man, still fiddlin' with his wheel, noticed a colored man with a team of horses comin' across the field. The man saw the problem an' took an awl from a small toolbox he had under the seat of his wagon. Soon the wheel was on with a makeshift pin. The man was a sharecropper who lived down the road apiece. He invited the salesman to his home, where he promised to replace the axel pin with a new one he had in his barn. Once at the sharecropper's home, he replaced the pin as promised, an' his wife fixed the salesman up with a sack lunch to take with him on his way. Of the three men, who would you say was a neighbor?" Asked Mel.

His question was met with silence.

"The colored man was a neighbor cause he was the only one who helped," answered Billy.

"That's right, Honey," Momma assured with a pat to the head, acknowledgin' his young wisdom, deciferin' between right an' wrong. "You're sayin' a neighbor is any one ta cross your path?" Uncle Joe asked.

"Me? No, not me. Jesus said it, Joe, in the tenth chapter of Luke, in the parable of the Good Samaritan. I've found it a good way to live."

"It's a good way fer all of us ta live," seconded the Pastor as he stood on the frin'e of our group behind Aunt Lee an' Uncle Joe.

We begin ta clean up the afternoon's gaiety, as bowls an' dishes were collected from the tables. Chairs an' tables were folded, an' the horseshoe pits retired 'til next year. We packed into the wagon ta start the short journey home. It had been a great day. Just as Pa was 'bout ta lead Blue back towards the road, Mr. Moyer come a-runnin' up ta us.

"Thanks so very much fer the invitation ta sit with y'all today. Why I just had a wonderful time."

"It was good of you ta sit with us," Momma smiled.

"Keep practicin' throwin' those shoes, an' next year Mel will toss me over fer you as a partner, an' the two of you will win hands down!" Pa laughed.

"Come by my place tomorrow. I'm gonna butcher a beef, an' I want you ta get some," Mr. Moyer offered.

Pa smiled an' looked at Mel, then he looked back at Mr. Moyer an' said. "Thank-you neighbor, the afternoon okay?"

"Sure, that'll be just fine," Mr. Moyer confirmed.

It was a great ride; we sang songs all the way home. Momma had a pretty voice, at times, she sung in the choir. Both Mel an' Pa sang along, but they both needed ta keep their voices soft. The softer, the better, Billy would say. That night as Momma helped us into bed, Little Bill said his prayers an' hugged on her neck.

"You know, Momma, I like Mr. Moyer now. I'm not scared of him any more. An' not just 'cause he's givin' me a puppy an' all."

"That's good, Billy. Mr. Moyer seems like he's goin' ta be a good friend."

Momma turned down the lamp an' left the room. I rolled over an' reached out ta touch my first place ribbon made of silk that lay on the table next ta my bed. Pa an' Mel's muffled voice's carried up to my second-story bedroom window. Try as I may, I couldn't make out the words. I could tell it was a friendly, end-of-a-good-day conversation, broken up from time ta time with quiet laughter. They sat out on the back porch fer a long time. I found myself wakin' up ta Pa's footsteps comin' up the stairs ta bed. I reached out in the darkness, lightly strokin' the silkiness of what had proved ta be a great day.

Chapter 8

Monday was a school day, as well as a workday. We were up, out, an' on our way. The excitement of yesterday had a spring in my step. Little Bill had a hard time keepin' up, ta an' from school. When we got home, we found Pa an' Mel finishin' up a workbench Pa had wanted fer a long while. It was long an' heavy; they could hardly move it ta where Pa wanted it.

"Next time we'll build it closer ta where we want it ta end up," Pa said after haulin' it across the barn.

"No arguments from me," Mel assured. "I'm gonna go an' start changin' a few of those fence posts," Mel said.

"Why don't you take a break?" Pa asked.

"A change is just as good as a break!" Mel said. "Hi, you two. Good day at school?"

"It was fine," I replied. "Dorothy wore her ribbon ta school. She was mad I didn't. I declare she strutted her stuff like that red rooster over there."

I was proud of my prize; the fact was I fergot ta

wear my ribbon. I couldn't just put it on now...I'd look like a copycat. Mel headed t'wards the road, shovel in hand. I looked ta the door that led ta the shed where Mel was spendin' his nights. I would hate ta sleep in there. He had cleaned it up, but still the idea'r'r of sleepin' almost inside the barn made me shudder. Then I thought, 'Jesus was born in a barn.' As I looked 'round an' filled my nostrils with the fragrance that accents a barnyard, I had a new insight ta my Savior as seen through the eyes of a child. Pa was finishin' up knockin' the sharp corners off the bench with san'paper. Billy stayed an' helped Pa; I headed ta the road where Mel was fixin' ta put in a new fence post. When I got there, Mel was stan'in' by a post.

"You come ta help me?" he smiled.

"You think this post needs changin'? It looks pretty good ta me."

"Well, Pumpkin, this post is like a lot of peoples' lives." He patted the old post. "It looks good from the outside straight an' tall. It looks similar ta the other posts up an' down the road. It even feels strong an' hard." Mel squeezed the top of the old post.

"But when you get ta the inside of the body, you discover that it's rotten an' decayed where the eye can't see. It's time ta trade the old fer the new."

Mel gave that post a shove; it splintered an'

crumbled at the base. The insects an' weather had eaten away at it, an' it was no longer of any use.

"You see, Pumpkin, only Jesus can heal us from the inside." Mel knelt down an' picked up some of the rotten wood dust, rubbed it between his fin'ers, an' blew it away. "That's what God does with sin when you show it to Him an' confess it. He just blows it away."

Mel smiled, picked up his shovel, an' started to dig away at the rotten wood an' level out the ground. Then he began to dig a new hole an' cover the memory of the old post with fresh dirt. "How many of these you gotta do?" I asked, lookin' down the post row.

"You see how these three posts are set kinda low in this ditch?" Mel asked.

"Yes."

"This ditch holds water, an' the water is what caused these posts to rot out sooner than those on the high ground," Mel explained. "Replacin' these will do it."

"Mr. Mel," I asked. "Do you hate stayin' in the shed?"

He began ta laugh. "What made you think of that?"

"Well, it's pretty dark at night, an' there's bugs an' snakes, an'...it's dark."

"I like it 'cause it's quiet an' clean, an' at night

it's dark. I'm very thankful fer a roof over my head."

"Have you ever lived in a house?" I asked.

Now he really started ta laugh! "Child, I have lived in many houses, I've slept in a few barns, an' under a few bridges. Hey! 'Member that doesn't make me a horse or a troll! So don't go tell anyone I am."

Deep down, I was afraid Mel was gettin' tried of our shed, an' someday I'd wake up ta find he moved along ta greener pastures an' softer beds. Now don't get me wrong, I never heard him complainin', not once. But you never know.

"Child, I'm very content where I put my head every night, don't you worry 'bout me."

"How's those posts comin'?" Pa asked as he came up ta us. "This one was in a big need of changin'," Pa said as he rolled the old post with his foot. "These three here need changin' out, an' the rest are fine."

"They was rotten from the inside, Pa," I informed him as a matter of fact.

"I can see that, Darlin'. They were pretty far gone," Pa agreed.

"Mel said people can be rotten on the inside just like these posts."

"Well, I reckon he's right 'bout that, Sweet Pea." Pa was still studyin' the post.

"I was gonna toss those on the burn pile," Mel told Pa.

"That'll be fine, thanks."

"You know who I thought was like this fence post? Mr. Moyer. I thought he was rotten inside, an' he fed children ta his dogs..."

"Child! Where did you ever come up with such foolishness!"? Pa asked, kinda shocked.

"Oh, It was somethin I heard," I explained.

"Don't you ever go 'round repeat nonsense like that!" Pa warned.

"Those are hurtful words. Now go back ta the house an' see if your Momma can use some help. Do you have any homework?" he questioned sternly.

"No, sir, I don't. Pa, I didn't say I believed what people was sayin'."

"Fine, you git on ta your Ma." His tone was a bit more soft.

Mel nodded a silent farewell as I started back towards the house. Pa wasn't often upset with me, an' I didn't like it when he was. Now when Billy was in the soup, I could sit down, drink a little tea, enjoy the show. But havin' Pa or Momma mad or disappointed in me was like bein' crushed, by havin' a big rock rolled over my chest. I slowly walked to the house, knowin' I had ta tell Momma why Pa sent me ta help her. Now she was goin' ta be upset too! I should have never listened ta those schoolyard yarns. Children bein' eaten by dogs, like adults wouldn't have put a stopped ta it. I only had myself ta blame sharin' children's whispers with grown-ups.

Billy was playin' in the yard, an' Momma was hangin' out some wash. I slowly walked up ta Momma. The smell of oven-fresh, baked goods swirled with the motion of the backyard breeze. "Pa said fer me ta see if I could help you," I said quietly.

Momma searched my face fer a clue as ta why Pa sent me ta her. "Why did your Pa send you ta me, Eula Mae?" she inquired.

"I said somethin that upset Pa," I admitted, "but I didn't mean nothin' by it. I was just sayin' somethin' I heard," I explained.

I told Momma why Pa had sent me over. I felt bad, I didn't want Mel ta think I was bein' mean ta Mr. Moyer. Momma let me hang out the rest of the wash after a good "talkin' to" 'bout spreadin' gossip. Little Bill overheard the scoldin' I got. He let me know I had better not cause him no trouble 'bout gettin' that pup. I was pretty much in everyone's doghouse. After hangin' out the wash, I just wan'ered 'round the backyard chasin' grasshoppers. Pa walked by me on the way into the house. He placed his hand on my head as he walked by.

"Did you see your Ma?" he asked.

"Yes, sir," I answered.

"I need a glass of water," he said as he climbed the stairs. The screen door stretched up an' snapped shut.

I saw Mel comin' from the road. He must be needin' a glass of water, too. I ran into the house ta get a glass fer Mel. Momma was already taken care of that fer Pa.

"Can I carry that out fer you, Pa?"

"Sure, take it on out ta Mel. He needs ta wet his whistle," Pa said.

"He's worked up a bit of a thirst."

I walked the cool glass of water out towards Mel. I was tryin' ta figure out how ta say I didn't mean nothin' 'bout what I said concernin', Mr. Moyer. I just couldn't have Mel thinkin' bad of me.

"Hey, is that fer me?" Mel smiled.

"Sure is. You looked kinda thirsty comin' down the road."

'Now that's pretty considerate," I thought. Now how ta bring up Mr. Moyer?

"Mr. Mel, you know I didn't mean anythin' 'bout what I said 'bout Mr. Moyer, don't you?"

"Pumpkin, now don't you fret 'bout that. I know you got a good heart, an' you was just repeatin' stories you heard tell."

'Why couldn't Pa had just figured that?' I thought.

"You just missed your opportunity."

Mel lifted the glass to his lips an' started to tilt the bottom of the glass to the sky.

"Missed what opportunity?" I questioned, never

wantin' ta miss out on anythin'.

"Well, the opportunity belongs to anyone who can talk. It's the opportunity to squash tales, lies, an' hurtful words. It's a great power we have, to allow painful thin's we hear to die by never repeatin' 'em again.

If we repeat those thin's we hear, we let those words an' thoughts go on livin'. We need to discern whether or not them words, an' things we hear, we are worthy of life. A good rule of thumb is if you hear somethin' good 'bout someone, somethin' that makes you smile, an' want that person to be your friend, those are words that are worthy of life. If you hear thin's that are not flatterin', then you most likely shouldn't be repeatin' 'em. Now why couldn't Pa explain it like that, 'steada just tellin' me "not ta repeat nonsense" an' sendin' me ta Momma ta hang out clothes? I'm thinkin' Mel should have some children of his own.

"I understan', an' I will be mindful of what I say in the future," I promised.

"I'm sure you will, Pumpkin. I think I might get me another glass of water."

"I'll get it." I snatched the glass from his hand before he could answer. I was up the back steps an' standin' at the sink pumpin' a glass of water.

"Is that fer Mel?" Pa asked.

"Yes, sir."

"Tell him I'm gonna head over ta Mr. Moyer's. He's got some beef he's slaughtered today, an' he offered us some. So I'll be takin' some bread, biscuits an' a pie your Ma baked, an' bring home some meat."

Mel nursed that glass of water as he put up the tools he had used. Pa hitched up Blue an' headed over ta Mr. Moyer's. Billy played Pa's shadow.

The old woman thought out loud, "Who can understan' the promptin' of the Holy Spirit's call? Is it a sudden flash of lightnin' in a clap of thunder? Or could it be a whisper carried through bush an' branch fer only your ears?"

I walked back ta that stand of woods behind the house. I climbed the ridge an' sat near the place Billy had tumbled into the creek. I began ta ponder. I felt a tug at my heart; I felt as if God was sayin' "sit closer to me, Eula Mae." I didn't know how ta, but I knew it felt right. I prayed that afternoon that Jesus would stay with me always. My Sunday school teacher told us we had ta believe He died fer our sins; an' was raised from the dead, an' sits on the right hand of the Father in heaven. That there was nothin', we could ever do that would be good enough ta git us ta heaven. So I believed. I believed as a child believes with all my heart an' hope'n, that Jesus was the truth. I believed 'cause Momma believed, an' I was sure Pa believed, an' the Reverend told us ta believe. All the grown-ups I knew went ta church. They must have believed, or they wouldn't be there. I knew Mel believed.

I was excited an' scared. I had done somethin' I knew was important without askin' permission. I had often prayed an' talked ta God, but I had never asked Him ta be with me always. I sat there, in my special place, alone in my thoughts, but not feelin' lonely. I saw Momma, through the trees, walk out of the house an' look 'round. Mel came out from the barn an' pointed in my general direction. I ran toward the house, through the woods, an' over the creek, across the cotton patch, an' into our property carryin' a secret in my heart.

"Your Ma is lookin' fer you, girl. You'd better git on in the house."

Mel's friendly advice quickened my steps. I bounded up the stairs an' straight into the kitchen.

"Honey, could you get this table set? I'm runnin' a little behind, an' I need some help."

"Yes, Momma."

Little Bill an' Pa weren't long, an' Momma fried us up some thick juicy steaks fer dinner. Mr. Moyer was gonna smoke the rest of the meat an' give us some more once it cured.

"This is sure tasty," Mel complimented Momma.

"We can thank Mr. Moyer fer this meal."

Momma deflected the praise as usual.

"He was surprised you sent those baked goods along with me. He wasn't expectin' anythin' today. I'll bet they were eaten before I got home!" Pa laughed.

"I suspect he eats pretty plain."

"Do we have a pie?" Billy asked. "Mr. Moyer offered us some of his, but Pa said no."

"We don't have any pie, but we do have some cobbler," Momma offered.

It was a good dinner, good food, family, Mel, an' I had a light an' happy heart.

Chapter 9

A full day at school was more than I could take; I was ready fer that long walk home. When we ran down the schoolhouse steps we saw we'd get a rare treat! Uncle Joe was sittin' there in his wagon. He had been in town an' it worked out he was passin' the school as we let out. Janey, Dorothy, Billy, an' I jumped in the wagon. A few children tagged along, 'til Uncle Joe hollered at 'em ta steer clear of his wheels.

"I don't want ta be takin' any flattened children home ta their parents," he told 'em.

Some of the children from school thought Uncle Joe was part Indian. He had a real red complexion, an' kinda squinty eyes. Once some children were passin' by his house when he was workin' on the roof. He let out an Indian war cry an' chased 'em all down the road. He laughed 'bout that fer years. I reckon that's where the rumor started. Uncle Joe took us home an' stopped ta visit awhile. He, Pa an' Mel sat beneath a tree talkin' 'bout the cotton crop, aphids, flea hoppers, boll weevils, an' how dry it had been. Pa an' Uncle Joe were a little concerned. Mel said the rains would fall.

That night I awoke in the dark ta what I thought was the sound of bacon fryin' in a pan. It was raindrops hittin' our tin roof. I loved that sound. I lay there wonderin' if Mel's hopin', wishin', or prayin' had caused the heavens ta open. I still couldn't figure him out, but life was good with him 'round. Late the next afternoon, I was throwin' some feed ta the chicks an' watchin' 'em dart 'round in their pen. Now one of Billy's jobs was walkin' the cotton rows lookin' fer bugs or eggs on the young leaves fer Pa. I noticed he was down at the edge of the field where the creek winds out of the woods. Momma was cookin' supper, Mel an' Pa were choppin' at the stump. All of a sudden, Billy comes a tearin' across the field screamin' his lung's out. I couldn't understan' him. He caught Pa's attention. Pa stopped choppin', put down the ax an' started slowly towards Billy.

"Snake! I got bit!" he was cryin' an' scared.

"What kinda snake boy?" Pa asked as Billy ran into his arms.

"Copperhead!" he shouted.

Mel took off towards where Billy had been stan'in'. Pa pulled up Billy's pant leg ta find the bite mark. I moved closer ta see. Ma came out of the house dryin' her hands ta see what was goin' on.

"Billy got bit by a snake! He thinks it was a copperhead," I said as Momma got closer. Her look of concern got me scared.

"Where did he get bit?" Momma asked

"Right here," Pa pointed out.

There were two little holes in little Bill's ankle. A dribble of blood trailed downward from both. I began ta cry. Mel was on the run back ta where we were. Pa picked up Billy an' headed ta the house. Momma took my hand.

"He's gonna be okay. You just hush. Billy will scare worst if'n you're cryin'."

Pa laid Billy in the downstairs back room on the wicker sofa. Mel came into the room where we were all gathered.

"I'm pretty sure it was a copperhead. I found a half dozen or so babies. They had the right bandin' an' yellow tails."

Billy's leg was already swellin' up.

"It burns, Momma; it burns."

"I know, Honey, it'll be alright. I'll put a cool cloth on it ta help the swellin'."

"Annie," Mel interrupted. "You shouldn't put anythin' on it; just let the wound bleed. Don't cut it or try suckin' out the poison. It's best if he just lies still."

"I'm goin' ta get Doc Horne," Pa said as he walked

out of the room.

"Momma," Billy sobbed. "Can I have some water? It burns so bad!"

Momma looked at Mel. Mel shook his head no.

"We'll wait 'til Doctor Horne gets here, Honey. He'll know what's best."

Mel looked at Momma an' suggested a wrappin' ta go on Billy's leg so that the poison couldn't spread. Momma, as gently as she could, removed his pants, all the time tellin' him he was her brave little boy.

"Not too tight," he warned.

Billy continued ta cry. His leg was still swellin', an' he seemed ta have a hard time catchin' his breath. His leg was puffy like a big old yellow squash.

Mel went out ta the back ta help Pa hitch up Blue. Pa had already thrown the saddle on Blue. Blue wasn't happy 'bout it, but Pa was not too patient today. In a snap, he was ridin' down the road ta fetch Doc Horne. Momma was kneeln' beside the sofa's edge strokin' Billy's hair when Mel came back in. Billy was cryin' softly now an' complained 'bout not seein' so clear. Momma told him ta close his eyes an' rest as she carefully laid her hand on his chest ta help regulate his breathin'. I stood in the doorway feelin' helpless. I wasn't seein' too good either; the tears kept flowin' down my cheeks. Momma smiled at me as she tended Billy. Mel placed his hand on my shoulder.

"He's goin' to be fine, he'll be sore a few days, but he'll be fine."

I knew then Billy would be back pesterin' me before the week was out. Still, I was anxious ta see what Doc Horne had ta say. Mel motioned me ta the kitchen, where the tators Momma was peelin' were turnin' brown in the sink.

"Maybe we should go ahead an' git supper cooked so your Ma can sit with Billy. It'll be a bit before your Pa gits back. There should be somethin to put on the table."

I told Momma not ta worry, Mel an' I had the supper goin'. Billy just lay there moanin'.

"My leg's on fire!" he cried.

I returned ta find Mel peelin' an' slicin' up the tators. He also had some lard meltin' in a fry pan.

"I'm gonna fry up these potatoes, an' some chicken, your Ma, was gonna cook. Why don't you heat up those beans an' set the table. 'Member the Doc will be here, so set a place fer him."

I found this so unreal. I was cookin' with Mel! Men never cooked unless they were fixin' BBQ or deep fryin' catfish or steamin' up mudbugs an' shrimps. I could hear Momma singin' softly ta Billy, an' him cryin'. I set the table an' put a heat on the beans. Mel was fryin' everythin' in sight, seemed he had been in a kitchen or two. It wasn't long before

I heard Blue come trottin' into the yard. Mel asked me ta watch the chicken while he went out ta put up Blue fer Pa. No sooner did Mel go out, Pa ran in. His little girl standin' at the stove was a sight, but not enough ta slow him down. He disappeared into the back room.

When Pa went into the room little, Bill cried all the more. I took the chicken out of the grease an' drained it like I watched Momma do a hundred times before. I covered it with a fryin' pan lid so's ta keep it warm. Mel came into the kitchen. He looked 'round an' smiled at the recognition I had handled everythin' in his absence.

"Well, I reckon you are goin' ta make someone a fine wife someday," Mel said with a smile.

"You, too," I giggled.

Mel gave me a shocked look, as if he couldn't believe his ears. Just then, Momma came out of the back room ta check in on us.

"Oh my, y'all are lookin' ta take my job!"

"How's Billy doin'?" Mel asked.

"The Doc is on his way. He said he's never known anyone ta die from a copperhead bite, not even a child. That's not ta say we don't have us a sick little boy! Everythin' you said ta do was what Doc Horne said ta do. Thank-you, Mel."

"Not a'tall. I just knew a thing or two," Mel said.

"Eula, Mel, you two sit down an' go ahead an' eat.

Your Pa an' me will sit with Doc Horne once he's through lookin' Billy over."

Mel an' I sat down an' helped ourselves ta some supper. Neither of us felt much like eatin'.

"Let's pray."

Mel returned grace. "Lord God our Father, Creator of the heavens an' the ground we walk, we ask you to visit this home an' place your hand of comfort an' healin' on young Billy Gilbert. We ask you ta soften his pain, replace his fear with peace. Show this young child your mercy an' love. Ease his parents fears an' let 'em draw strength from you in this time. I pray fer his sister, that she may be a reflection of your tenderness to her younger brother. As always, we ask that your blessin' be on this food an' this home. Keep this family close to you as they journey through life, always lookin' to you, our Lord an' Savior. Amen."

I smiled at Mel. His prayer was an offerin' ta God from the deepest parts of his heart. The smells of the food before me made my mouth water. I was pretty proud of the deep golden tone my fried chicken had. All it needed was a little salt. Mel was kinda quiet; he had one eye on supper an' the other on the back room. It wasn't long before the sound of Doc Horne's buggy rolled up along side the house. Mel went out ta tend ta the Doc's rig. As the Doc entered the kitchen, he stopped an' took a deep breath.

"Well, had I known how good it smelled in here, I wouldn't have spent so much time stitchin' up Mr. Lewis's hand. Now, where's this young'un who went an' got himself bit?"

Doc Horne seemed ta come in an' take over, puttin' everyone at ease with his levity. He went back an' asked Billy had he bit the snake first? Cause copperheads tend ta steer clear of people.

"No, honest Pa, I didn't bite 'em!"

Sometimes Billy wouldn't know a funnin' unless it did bite him. The Doc examined his leg an' told Momma she could give Billy a bit of water. He cleaned the bite mark with alcohol, which filled our little kitchen, overpowerin' the smells Mel an' I created.

"He's goin' be fine. That leg will swell up to the knee, but if it swells higher, you come get me right away. He can eat, he may feel a bit queasy an' he make get some diarrhea, but that's normal."

The Doc's reassurances were comfertin' ta us all. Pa offered the Doc some supper while Momma sat with Billy. I brought Momma Billy's favorite book, The Swiss Family Robinson. She read it 'til he fell asleep. The Doc, Pa, Mel an' Momma sat 'round the table, just passin' time fer a few hours so the Doc could check Billy's leg again before leavin'. Mel retired ta the shed fer the evenin', Momma an' Pa were most grateful fer his help. As they tucked me in, they thanked me fer helpin', too. Pa said I fried up some good chicken! I told 'em Mel had prayed fer everyone at supper an' he helped in the kitchen. I couldn't take all the credit.

We all slept sound that night. There's nothin' like a hard day's work or a good scare that will cause you ta sleep like a pile of fieldstones. I laid there the longest time imaginin' life without my baby brother. I thought of that day when I thought I saw him lyin' in the creek with his life's blood ming'lin' with the current. That image has always remained with me. I no longer question it; I just thank God fer His mercies.

Chapter 10

The next day, Tuesday, I told an' retold the story of how my little brother almost died from bein' bit by a copperhead. An' how his leg was puffed up this mornin' like a balloon. I didn't let on how much he cried an' hollered. I didn't think everyone ought ta know all the details. He limped an' hobbled 'round fer days, till Pa told him he'd better stop babyin' his leg other wise he'd limp fer the rest of his life! Now I don't know if that was true, but little Bill was runnin' 'round shortly after that warnin'. From then on he carried a big stick an' beat the ground in front of him whenever he was checkin' the cotton plants fer bugs an' infestations. That Saturday mornin', Billy was still runnin' Momma ragged.

"Could you get me some water? Would you read ta me a bit? Do we have anythin' sweet?"

I will say, his leg was still swollen, but he was milkin' the situation fer every last drop.

"I thought Lincoln freed the slaves?" Pa said ta

Momma as she made her way up ta Billy's bed.

"Mr. Lincoln fergot 'bout me," Momma puffed out. "That child can think of more thin's fer me ta do!"

I think Momma was happy ta do all of them things. Her baby was safe in bed, an' she was grateful. There are times in life when gratefulness can be overwhelmin'. Moments when you're so thankful fer what, an' who you have, it's hard ta breathe ... funny how it takes almost losin' those things, an' those people ta make life so clear. This was one of those times fer my momma. She was always so strong, an' certain of what was right an' wrong. What it simply comes down ta, is a child-like faith.

"Billy, I want you ta get out an' get some fresh air. We can spread a blanket by one of the trees, or set out a foldin' chair," Momma called up the stairs.

"Your cousins are comin' over in a little while ta visit. You all can visit outside."

Now the reason Jane an' Dorothy were comin' over was 'cause Pa an' Uncle Joe were plannin' on buyin' more pigs. So they had ta build some more pens an' a hog barn. Momma wanted it built over at Uncle Joe's farm, but Pa said he was the one who'd be carin' fer it.

"You just build that stink house back away from my home, Otis! That smell is gonna wake us up every mornin'."

"Annie, we're gonna put it across the road on the Prichert property," Pa told her, tryin' ta easy her concerns.

"Oh, over near the ponds?" Momma asked.

"Yes, Darlin', over close ta the ponds, the smell won't bother you," Pa promised.

"Over by the ponds where there's been a gator livin' fer years?" Now Momma was not only soundin' a little bit mad, but a bit sassy!

"Those gators, they'll be eatin' bacon every mornin' fer breakfast!"

Momma was not happy. She'd have her say an' be done.

"Annie," Pa said firmly, "I'll be takin' care of the gators an' clearin' out that whole parcel. We're gonna raise hogs, we're gonna butcher an' sell 'em into the market. Cotton isn't gonna cut it alone; we need ta do this," he said softly.

It was over, Pa was headed in a direction, an' we all needed ta climb on his wagon fer the ride. Uncle Joe, Aunt Lee an' the girls were soon there. We were all lookin' over Billy's leg.

"Can I touch it?" Janey asked.

"Sure, go 'head," Billy insisted.

As soon as her finger begin ta stroke his taut, smooth skin I poked my finger into her side an' in a deep craggy voice shouted.

"Aauugggg!"

Both Janey an' Dorothy jumped. I guess they thought Billy's leg was goin' ta explode all over 'em. We laughed.

"Go on, touch it again," Billy told Janey.

She hesitated, but finally reached fer it. Before she could lay a finger on him I zapped her again! She gave me a shot ta the arm, but I was laughin' so hard, I didn't feel it. Pa, Uncle Joe an' Mel were stan'in' by the fence talkin'. Uncle Joe was leanin' on the fence. They seemed ta make a decision an' started walkin' towards the road.

"Let's go see where they're goin'," I said, so we trailed off behind 'em.

"Wait up!" Billy complained as he limped behind us.

"You don't have ta come, keep up or go sit down."

I got that from Pa. Billy's pace quickened. The men were headed across the road ta a piece of land Pa bought from ol' man Prichert. It was a little hilly, an' had two ponds with a couple of gators in 'em. That's why we weren't allowed ta fish it or chase frogs an' turtles there. There were a lot of trees, hickory, oaks, an' beechnut, even a couple of pecans. This parcel of property would have been hard ta farm 'cause of all the trees an' the ups an' downs.

Pa musta figured this land fer hogs all the time. We walked back towards the ponds, Billy kept a watchful eye out fer snakes, beatin' the ground with a stick he had picked up, Dorothy followin' him with a stick of her own. Janey plowed through the tall grass like a bull. Pa was pointin' out ta Mel an' Uncle Joe where he wanted ta build. He was plannin' on usin' the pond ta water the hogs. He wanted ta kill off the gators an' stock the pond with bream an' catfish. I heard him say they might someday sell some fish, too. Sell fish? When a body could just go down a catch 'em fer free? What's next? Sellin' water, I suppose. We walked that land an' circled the spring-fed ponds, no signs of snakes or gators.

"First thing is ta make sure the ponds are clear of gators," Pa said. "I

don't want ta be feedin' 'em bacon fer breakfast!"

Mel an' Uncle Joe laughed. Pa sure didn't laugh when Momma said

the same thing earlier.

"Then I thought we'd get Bob Johnson ta bring in his bushhog an' chop all this brush an' thick grass back."

Pa's plan was comin' together.

Have him go 'head an' till up the ground where we're puttin' the pens. Once the hog's git in 'em they'll keep that growth down. We'll leave those trees all in place ta shade them pigs an' give 'em a little added shelter, an' they'll eat up on the nuts.

"We'll put up small pens an' just keep eight ta twelve ta a pen. What do you think Mel?" Pa asked.

"I think you two are gonna give hogs a good name, an' sounds like someone will be shovelin' a lot of manure," smiled Mel.

"Well, I need ta ask you this Mel. Are you gonna be here awhile? This is a big deal. I'll be needin' ta tend the fields, keep up the maintenance of the farm, garden, an' start this whole big boy. I'm gonna need help, we're gonna need help, ta put all this together. We'll be lookin' ta you."

Pa stated it plain, there would be a lot of work an' Mel's back was needed ta share the load. I was afraid of the answer 'cause this would be the time ta leave if that was a notion.

"I'll be happy ta stay 'round an' help y'all with your deal," was Mel's answer. "By the way what is the diffrence 'tween a pig an' o' hog?"

"Pigs git fed, hogs git slaughtered." Uncle Joe defined.

I wanted ta hoot an' holler, but this was grown-up conversation, an' I

needed ta be a little pitcher with big ears. As we walked back ta our house, I was so happy Mel would be stayin' on awhile. Settin' up a hog farm was goin' ta take a bit of doin', but Pa had a plan, an' Mel was gonna help! We headed back across the road ta our place. Billy's limp got worst the closer ta Momma we got. Me an' the girls played cards. Billy sat with the women soakin' up as much lovin' an' pity as he could. While men were off talkin' 'bout pigs an' pens an' such, Janey toldme how James an' David Horton, the twins who lived across from thepreacher's house, painted their little sister black an' tried ta sell her ta thecolored family that lives in the woods back behind the church! They called the colored man who lives there Moses, on account of his white beard an' hair. Moses brought the little girl an' her brothers ta the preacher's house.

He didn't know who these children belonged to but figured the preacher would. The preacher took 'em all home, an' the twins got the tar whipped out of 'em. They scrubbed that girl raw, an' she still got paint on her! Uncle Joe said they'd got more money fer her if they left her white, I said that was a mean thing say. He'd say stuff like that every now an' again. My pa was raised by the same woman, an' I never heard a mean thing come from his mouth 'bout man nor beast 'cause o' their color or religion. I prayed fer Uncle Joe's heart that he only judged others by the way God judges us.

"Ma," Dorothy called, "can I git somethin' ta eat?"

"No, we'll be eaten lunch in a bit," Aunt Lee answered.

"I know," I said quietly, "follow me."

We got up from the stairs. We walked toward the pump, then back towards the house, then towards the men, an' then back behind the barn.

"Where are we goin'?" Dorothy asked once out of earshot.

"I know where there's a wild rhubarb patch," I answered.

"I love rhubarb!" Janey giggled. "Where's it at?"

"Over just inside the woods. We can each get a stalk," I said, wantin' ta save the patch fer special occasions.

We walked along the worn path Billy an' I had made, 'til we came upon my personal little patch of sourness. Next ta sugar cane stalks, rhubarb was my next favorite chew.

"This is pretty good!" Dorothy said with a surprise.

"I like 'em young like this," Janey said as her face twisted from the taste.

I thought 'bout tellin' 'em how Billy an' I first met Mel back here, but then I'd have ta swear 'em ta secrecy. Besides, I could come off lookin' like I got a pump with no water comin' out.

"I hear Ma callin'," Janey said, an' with that, we were off.

The men were now sittin' 'round the outside table. Momma an' Aunt Lee were in the kitchen gettin' lunch ready.

"You girls get that table set an' see what everyone wants ta drink," Momma called from the kitchen window.

Soon we was takin' lunch together, the adults at one end, an' the children on the other. We all sat along a table Pa an' Paw Paw had built. They called it a harvest table. It was long an' would hold our bounty at harvest time. It was one of the last thin's Pa an' his pa did together. Both my Paw Paw Bill an' Mimi died of the flu in 1909; they was Pa's folks. Now my Ma's pa no one ever talked 'bout. I figured he run off or was in jail. Since her ma, Gran'ma Ada, died when Momma was young, Momma come ta live with Aunt Lee's people, on accounta Aunt Lee's ma an' Momma's ma were sisters.

I was listenin' in on the adult conversation. I heard Uncle Joe tellin' Pa they was gonna have ta buy a truck. Pa wasn't interested in spendin' a half a year's wages ta go faster.

"Otis, we're gonna need a truck ta get those hogs ta market. If we got our selves a truck, we can take those hogs up ta Vicksburg directly an' sell 'em fer top dollar. We can grow our own feed, an' with all those nut trees, the hogs will eat good. Why we can even sell manure if we want," Uncle Joe concluded.

"Sometimes I think your sellin' it ta me," Pa laughed.

"Otis, I think you ought ta be listenin' ta your brother. He sounds like he's thought this out," Momma said. "Not ta say you haven't, but the thoughts of two brains puttin' out idea'rs needs twice the consideration."

"Eula, go in the house an' find me some paper an' a pencil," Pa directed.

I got up, takin' one last bite of beans an' jumped the stairs an' into the house. I scurried to the kitchen cabinet. I found a pencil, but the paper was another matter. I went into the front room, ta the hutch cabinet an' began openin' drawers I had never looked into. Momma kepy special thin's in those drawers, thin's children don't need ta be handlin', linens, photos, important papers. My search fer a piece of writin' paper was takin' longer than it should. As I was openin' the last drawer in the cabinet, Momma came in the room.

"There's nothin' in that drawer fer you! Shut it an' don't go in places you shouldn't be!" Momma said sharply.

I was a bit taken back at her tone; it scared me. I thought I had done somethin' wrong. I quickly stood up.

Pa asked me ta git him a piece of paper an' I couldn't find any, in the kitchen cabinet, so I was searchin' everywhere ta find a piece, I explained.

"I was usin' the paper out in the back room. Go git it an' bring it ta your pa," she said in a softer, more kinder way.

As I walked by, she put her hand on my shoulder

an' kissed my head.

"I didn't mean ta be sharp with you, Honey."

"That's okay, Momma, I'll get the paper an' go directly out ta Pa."

As I sat down at the table ta finish up my meal, I wondered what could be in that drawer that would make my Momma so angry. We finished up an' cleared the table. The men threw horseshoes while the women cleaned up. That never set with me too well. Janey wanted ta go see where Billy got bit Dorothy wanted ta play cards or draw. We did neither 'cause Pa sent us ta the garden ta pick weeds.

"Ya didn't pick weeds this mornin', so you'll pick now. If'n this was the middle of summer, it'd be hotter than blazes out here. You'd be wishin' you'd got up early in the coolness of the day ta git these kinda of chores done."

"Janey, Dorothy, you both git out there an' help your cousin," Uncle Joe hollered.

So we picked up one row an' down the other. Little Bill sat in the shade with his leg propped up, scratchin' it with a stick, lookin' over at me from time ta time, ta see if I noticed he was sittin' in the shade with his leg propped up, scratchin' it with a stick. That boy didn't know it, but his goose was cooked. Sooner than later, I was gonna get him good. Pretty soon, Aunt Lee an' Uncle Joe took their leave. We waved at the girls til the wagon was out of sight. Pa walked the cotton fields, checked the ground fer moisture, an' the plants fer bugs. Ma was in the house, doin' a little mendin'. Momma had Billy in the kitchen cleanin' out the kitchen drawers an' wipin' down the cabinets. Seems she got him before I did. Mel was nowhere ta be seen. I finished throwin' the weeds in a pile where they'd dry out an' then Pa would burn 'em. When I turned 'round, Mel was sittin' at the harvest table alone. I could see Pa at the far end of the field.

"Come here, Pumpkin, I've got somethin fer you," Mel called ta me.

"What is it?" I asked with great curiosity.

I walked over ta see Mel had carved out of wood a pendant like I saw at Marie's general store. There were three crosses; the center cross was a bit bigger than the other two. The one ta the left of the center was slightly bigger than the one ta the right. The right one was attached by the horizontal bar of the cross. It was in the lowest position of the three. The one ta the left was nestled under the center cross's bar. It hung from a piece of red silk pipin'. I had never owned a piece of jewelry before, just some ribbons, an' an old cigar band once. This wasn't silver or gold, but it was as precious ta me.

"Come on, let's see if it fits."

Mel had me turn 'round as he hung the pendant 'round my neck.

"Oh, Mr. Mel, thank-you so much! It's the prettiest pendant I ever saw! I'm gonna wear it ta church tomorrow! I gotta show Momma."

I started ta run away, then turned back ta give Mel a big hug an' kiss as he sat in the chair.

"Now your Ma an' Pa haven't seen it yet, but they said it was okay ta make it fer you, so be sure ta thank 'em."

Momma thought it was the prettiest pendant she'd ever seen, too. I think she was a bit jealous. Then I ran out ta the field an' caught up with Pa ta show him.

"That Mel, he's sure gotta talent with that wood carvin'. That is the most intricate work I ever laid my eyes on. That is one piece of wood. I mean, it's not glued. You need ta keep this in a special place, so it doesn't git broke. Never wear it when you're playin' or roughhousin' 'round."

"I won't, Pa. This is fer church an' special occasions," I assured, understan'in' Pa was just so impressed by Mel's craftsmanship. I later found out Mel had carved both little Bill an' myself a rabbit. One was a girl; an' one was a boy. The detail of those creatures was incredible. They stood 'bout three inches high. The hard, bold, muscular edges gave a definite manly appearance ta Billy's. The soft an' rounded carvin' gave Maggie, my rabbit, the look an' form of a female. Mel had placed each hair on their little bodies with the edge of a graver. Now I knew what he'd been doin at night when he retired fer the evenin'.

Chapter 11

I woke early Sunday mornin, sittin on my bed, holdin my pendant, which I had placed on the nightstan' fer the evenin'. I could hardly wait ta show it off. There were plenty of oohs an' ahhs before the service. Even the men folk came up an' admired my gift. I guess Mel turned as many shades of red a body can. He was complimented as if he was a proud papa of a newborn son.

Many asked how he came by this talent. 'God given" was his answer time an' time again. Billy told everyone 'bout his rabbit Mel carved, wishin' he had brought it. He was able ta show off his copperhead bite, which also was met with some oohs an' ahhs. When we got home Momma made us somethin' ta eat before sendin' us ta play. She was gonna rest a spell. Pa asked us if we wanted ta go over ta the ponds an' see if we could scare up a few bream, maybe even a bass, if'n the gator hadn't eaten 'em all. Mel had already dug some red worms; Pa had three cane poles ready ta go. Billy an' I would be sharin'. As we got closer ta the first pond, I suddenly stopped.

"What's that?" I jumped.

"What?" Billy asked as he took two paces back, stick in hand.

"I saw somethin' slitherin' through the grass over there."

I watched Billy as he peered through the thick grassy scrub. I hadn't seen a thin' but I wanted ta share that pole as little as possible.

"You know those cottonheads like that damp, moist earth like by a creek or a pond," I whispered so snakes an' fathers couldn't hear. Billy hung back a bit, while Pa, Mel an' I tried ta see if here was anythin' in the pond worth a hoot. After just a moment, I mean the ripples hadn't even made it ta the bank, Pa's bobber disappeared. Pa was lookin' back at Billy.

"I'd take that bobber back ta the store if I were you, it just sunk," Mel joked.

Pa was caught off guard, thinkin' the pond was dead 'n all. As he started ta lift, the fish cut in a circle. Pa's pole bent towards the water as the fish dove deep ta the weeds. Pa smiled as he watched the fish dance beneath the water's surface. Billy was edgin' his way t'wards the bank, without lookin' at him I stomped the tall grass closest ta me as if ta ward off an unseen threat.

"He don't wanna come in!" Pa said as he lifted the bull bream from his watery home. As Pa was releasin' his catch, Mel's bobber vanished, an' then mine!

"Well it looks like were gittin' into some fish here. Eula, don't be tellin' any one 'bout these ponds! As far as you know, they're filled with gators."

"Can I catch a fish?" Billy asked.

"Come here, boy. You can fish with me," Pa beckoned.

We all caught fish - a half a dozen or so each! They was nine ta eleven inches each, which makes pretty good eatin'. Pa did find a slide trail where a gator would enter an' leave the water. We hadn't seen one, but the trail was fresh.

"Now see this here," he said, pointin' to the trail. "This is why I don't let you two come down here alone. If I ever catch either of you two disobeyin' me 'bout this, I'll blister you so you can't sit down fer a week!" Pa warned us sternly. We would never come to the ponds on our own, with Pa ready ta beat us if'n we did. I know he's just scared of what might happen if a gator got us. A gator would grab you an' pull you in the water. Then take you ta the deepest part, cause he'd want ta drown ya. Then he'd tuck you up under a fall down of a tree or a brush pile, or maybe even 'neath the bank somewhere till you got all soft an' tender. Then he'd just rip off hulks 'til you were gone. At least that's how Uncle Joe tells it.

"We'll get a good fish fry outta there some evenin'," Pa promised as we walked back towards home. Little Bill kept up with Pa's every step.

"Mel, Annie wasn't gonna cook tonight. She's tuckered out. I'm just gonna make some sandwiches an' open a jar of pickles, nothin' fancy."

"Hey, don't worry I can eat out in the shed or at the table in the yard," He insisted.

"Oh no, I wasn't meanin' anythin' like that. I'm just sayin' I won't be makin' up a hot meal tonight."

"That's fine, if I can help, just ask. I was a short order cook fer a time. I can fry, bake, poach, or roast anythin' that grows, swims, or runs!"

Mel went back to the shed to rest his eyes fer a while.

"I'm gonna walk the cotton field a spell. I didn't get through it yet this week," Pa said as he went ta put up the poles in the barn.

"Can I go with you Pa?" Billy asked.

"Sure, boy. How's that leg holdin' up?" Pa checked ta see if he'd be carryin' little Bill home.

"When you go in the house you be quiet, Eula." Pa reminded me Momma was restin'.

When I went up the back porch stairs I stepped ta the side so's not ta creak the planks. I held the screen door so it wouldn't slam shut. I walked through the downstairs on tip toes. I quietly snuck up stairs ta find Momma in bed asleep. Her bottle of medicine, Eve, on the nightstand beside her.

I crept down ta the front room, where out the window I saw Pa an' Billy walk the rows. I took a book from the shelf, sat on the floor an' begin ta read. My eyes left that book an' wandered over ta the hutch. In particular, the bottom drawer. What could that drawer possibly hold that would upset my Momma so? I knew I shouldn't, but I had ta know, kinda like that cat that curiosity kill'd. I listened ta make sure there was no creakin' floorboards above me, as I inched my way over ta that uncertain drawer. I slid it open with such silence, peerin' into its depths, fearin' at any moment I would be discovered.

There I found only a box, a sin'le old shirt box. I strained my ears an' held my breath tryin' ta catch some evidence of my mother's consciousness. I placed the box on the floor in front of me an' slowly removed it's lid. I was surprised ta find it tightly packed. There was not a space left fer a sheet of paper. I discovered in this mystery box two brightly colored spinnin' tops. At first, I thought they were a surprise fer little Bill. Then I went on ta find a couple of neatly folded shirts an' a small pair of boy's leather shoes. There was some children's drawin's linin' the bottom of the box, as well as a leather school case ta carry pencils an' other supplies.

The most tellin' item was the leather marble bag with the name Lovus printed on the outside. Lovus was my older brother. I don't 'member much 'bout him, he died of pneumonia when I was 'bout two. My only clear memory is sittin' on his lap on a porch swin'. He never came ta my mind. Billy an' I never spoke of him, an' my parents never mentioned his name. I'm figurin' the pain was just too great. I 'membered Pa, Uncle Joe an' Mel talked 'bout Mr. Johnson losin' his boy when we was comin' home from fishin' at the river. It never occurred ta me 'bout Pa havin' lost his boy too.

I was just thinkin' how sometimes Momma would be off in her own thoughts, an' I'd interrupt her. I'd catch her with tears in her eyes, an' she'd hug me so hard I could hardly breathe. She might be tryin' ta make up fer all the hugs she missed out on givin' ta Lovus. Someday I'll have a child, an' I'll tell that youngun of the uncle he never met. An uncle who played with tops, an' marbles, an' was loved by his Pa an' Momma. I will tell him of the time I' membered sittin' in his uncle's lap, swin'in' on an old porch swin'.

I have no idea'r how long I sat there, thinkin' 'bout a mother's pain, my Momma's pain. There are two sides ta every bed. The joy, an' the hurt. I guess you can't take one unless you're willin' ta accept the other. Billy was born pert'ner the time Lovus passed. I guess God saw fit ta give my Momma and Pa a little bundle of hope in a time where they had none.

I placed everythin' back the way I found it. Away from children's pryin' eyes.

Momma was still asleep. Pa an' Billy were comin' in from the field. I was feelin' sad. I can see why Momma wanted me ta stay outta that drawer. It's hard ta be left behind when someone goes away. Momma won't see Lovus 'til she steps into Glory. What a day that'll be! Knock, knock, knock. Someone gently rapped at the backdoor. I got up ta answer it.

"Hi, Mr. Mel, Pa's walkin' in from the field." I directed his attention behind him.

"No, Pumpkin, I wanted to return this glass your Ma let me use last night. You okay? You look a bit taken back," Mel said as he studied my face.

"I'm fine, I'm just doin' a little readin', that's all," I assured him. "I liked wearin' my cross today. Thank you, again," I said, changin' the subject.

"Miss Melba thought it was the prettiest thin' she ever saw. Mrs. Culton wanted ta know if you was sellin' 'em."

"No, that's a one of a kind you got there," Mel promised me. "Tell your Ma thanks very much fer the use of the glass."

He left ta piddle 'round the yard, maybe pitch a

few shoes, no that'd be too noisy fer, Momma. Here comes Billy limpin' cross the yard. Pa was on his heels, hollerin' at him ta stop limpin'. I watched from the screen door.

"Boy, you keep up that limpin' an' you'll end up gimpin' fer the rest of your life! No more runnin fer you, an' when it's time ta go swimmin', you'll just be able ta go in circles cause your right side will be so much stronger."

"Pa, it still hurts a bit. That's why I favor it."

"I'm tellin' you what ta expect. You need ta walk normal," Pa insisted.

"Okay, Pa, I will."

Now Billy would grow up ta be either on the stage or a martyr. I don't think martyrs make much money, so he'll probably try the stage. His little face grimaced an' shook with pain, an' defiance of pain with each step he took to prove ta Pa he was a son ta be proud of. After a half dozen paces or so, he looked ta Pa fer approval of his brave accomplishment. Pa smiled an' told him ta practice every day an' when Billy was walkin' straight as an arrow, Pa would teach him ta drive the wagon.

"An' when you an' Uncle Joe get your truck, will you teach me ta drive that. too?"

Billy was always one ta start the wheelin' an' dealin' early.

"Boy, you will probably own a truck before I ever

do. Eula, Honey, bring me a glass of water. I got some dust in my throat."

Billy went off ta the side of the house ta practice walkin'. I sat with Pa as he drank his water.

"How the crops doin?" I asked.

"Seem ta be just fine, growin', healthy, no bugs ta speak of," Pa answered, lookin' over the rim of his glass across his land.

"Hope it's a good crop. Gotta lot of work here this summer with settin' up this hog farm."

"Mr. Mel will help you. He's a good worker." I was bein' reassurin'.

"I know, Darlin', it'll all git done." Now Pa was bein' reassurin' ta me.

He gave me a hug an' went ta check on Momma. She had gotten up an' was relaxin' on the front porch. Pa sat an' they talked awhile. Mel, Billy, an' I made sandwiches an' took 'em on the front porch. We sat, an' talked, enjoyin' each other's company. Momma was enjoyin' bein' taken care of.

"There was this one time," Mel began, "I was standin' on this river bank in the middle of a little town where I was stayin'. It was a quaint town filled with shops an' people. Where we were stan'in', it was an eight-foot shear drop to the water. I was cleanin' my nails with a pocketknife a dear friend had given me as a gift. The man stan'in' next to me was from the church I was attendin'. He was the most fun lovin', an' at the same time most orneriest man I had ever come to meet. I believe his smile an' laugh had hid more tricks an' pranks than anyone would believe. He'd reach out an' shake your hand an' pinch you with the other; then a third hand would come from out of no where an' point out in which direction the culprit who just pinched you went."

We all laughed.

"Wouldn't you know, I dropped that pocketknife right into the river. Now the river was high an' runnin' fast. The bank we were stan'in' on cut in a ways from the main body of water when the river was lower, creatin' a nice little pool. Well, Dan's stan'in' there laughin' that I'd be cleanin' my nails over the water, an' hadn't had the sense God gave a church mouse to have taken two steps back. Now I can't just leave that knife at the bottom of the river, an' this joker is tellin' me all the time how that's the prettiest knife he ever saw. Bout a hundred an' fifty paces past the bridge; the bank sloped down to the river's edge. I took a stick an' laid it on the bank at the spot where I last saw my knife enter the water. I looked at Dan an' told him to keep an eye on me in case the current takes me away." 'Oh, sure, I'll keep an eye on you, I'll be right here when you get back."

"Well, now, I go down to a place I can git in the

water. I don't pull off my shoes 'cause that river is just filled with everythin' you could think of, an' I don't want to be cuttin' my foot. I stepped into this cold, rushin' water. It kinda took my breath away. All the time, I'm thinkin', 'What was I thinkin' 'bout, stand'in' so close to the river?' I stayed close to the shore as I slowly made my way upstream. The river's depth varied from waist to chest high, an' it was movin' fast. As I came from under the bridge, I could see the stick I had placed on the bank to mark my spot. Dan was nowhere to be seen. Why I could be floatin' down the river headed fer the dam an' who knows where Dan was. When I got to the mark, I slipped outta one of my shoes, an' started to feel 'round the riverbed in hopes of findin' my knife. At this point, I only went through with the search 'cause I found myself stan'in in a strong river, fully clothed in the middle of town, lookin' fer a knife that had probably been swept away by a current.

"I was a sight, standin' in the river in the middle of the day, an' my friend was gone! Then my toes, which were beginnin' to numb, felt the shape of what seemed to be my knife! I ran my toe down the length of the object an' found the pointy end of my blade. I couldn't believe it! Then a familiar face peeked over the edge of the bank. Where have you been?' I asked him. I could be drowned, fer all you know.

"Did you find it?" he asked.

"I told him yes. He told me no way 'round it. I was gonna have to go under water to get my knife. If I tried to hold on to it with my toes an' lift it up to my hand, an' the current caught it, all this would be fer nothin'. I had to go to the knife holdin' it all the while with my foot. Now, I was not happy, I had managed to keep my shoulders on up dry, but now I'd be baptized fer sure. I looked at Dan's smilin' face from above, enjoyin' the sight of my situation. I took a breath an' bent down to retrieve my prize. Finally, it was in my hand, fer it once was lost, an' now was found, just like the sheep in the parable. I spurted water from my mouth an' slung the hair to the side of my head. I opened my eyes, holdin' up the knife fer Dan to see!

"There he stood, his face hidden behind a box, a camera! While I had walked down the shoreline to climb in the river, an' slowly made my way up stream, he'd run into a store front no more than forty feet away. Bought a camera as quick as one, two, three! Got out of the store an' back to the river just as I was comin' up. He waited fer that prefect moment, an' SNAP! We all laughed so hard, I was sure Aunt Lee an' Uncle Joe would be rollin' up in their wagon ta see what kinda ruckus was goin on.

Pa looked at Mel.

"I'd like ta see that picture," he confessed.

"Dan said he'd always wanted a Brownie camera but needed a good enough excuse to buy one. I was it."

Mel could sure entertain us with one of his stories. Pa never told stories. I wasn't sure if he just wasn't any good at it, or maybe he couldn't share his stories with children. As I laid my head on the pillow that night, my thoughts was just stumblin' 'round. I prayed fer Momma an' Pa, an' the pain they must suffer every day, I prayed that I would be a good daughter, an' never cause 'em grief, cause I was sure they had had their fill. I changed positions time an' again unable ta find a place I could call comfortable. Momma musta heard the bedsprin's creakin' with every toss I made.

She crept inta my room ta check on me. I sat up in bed an' reached out ta her. In the stillness of the hour, she came ta the edge of my bed an' held me. I felt so safe an' protected. I shoved my face deep into her nightshirt. I never wanted ta let go. I wanted ta stay in her arms ferever, an' I believe at that moment, it was her wish, too.

"What is it, Honey? Why are you havin' such a hard time gettin" ta sleep?"

"I don't know. Would you just lay with me a while?"

"I sure will, Sugar. Now just close your eyes an' think of happy thoughts."

She wrapped her arms 'round my little body. I felt so small an' secure. I could feel her heartbeat, her warmth made me sleepy. I finally drifted off. I never realized she left 'til the next mornin'.

Chapter 12

It was the beginnin' of a new week. School was almost over fer the summer. There would be swimmin' at the culvert, playin' with the girls, fishin', an' lots of explorin'. We loved ta go explorin'. Explorin' was when you'd pack up thin's you need, a san'wich, an' Pa's old canteen full of water, some matches an' a huntin knife. Then we'd pick a direction an' walk lookin fer stuff. We'd find old cans, dead animals an' a shoe once back in the woods. How could a man lose his shoe an' not know it? We found a foxes' den, an' sat real quiet fer a long time an' spied her pups. If we really wanted ta do hard explorin' we'd brin' a shovel an' dig into mounds we found, Indian burial grounds!

Tommy Watkins older brother, Buddy, had once found Indian arrowheads by diggin' 'em up. He found pieces of old pottery, too! Momma said we shouldn't disturb their final peace. Pa never said nothin'. I loved the summers. There were more chores, but I didn't mind. I would sleep a little longer an' play a little harder. Life just seemed a little freer. The school day had seemed long. There were a couple of times I could've sworn I had ants in my pants. The warmer the weather the less I felt like bein' inside. I think most children feel that way, an' most mothers want those same young'uns out the door, too. When we got home from school we found Momma alone. Pa an' Mel had gone ta town with Uncle Joe ta order supplies they'd need ta build the pens. Momma said Uncle Joe had figured out everythin' they needed an' there was no sense in wastin' time.

"Are they orderin' a truck?" Billy asked.

"I wouldn't count on that, Sweetheart," Momma smiled.

"I want you two ta go out an' git your chores done, lickety-split."

Billy's limp was disappearin, 'ceptin' when chores were needin' done. Then he got ta favorin' that limb. Billy started over ta the water trough ta git some water ta pour in fer the hens.

"Billy, don't move," I whispered. "I think I saw a snake go under the trough. I'll water the animals, you go an' clean the coop."

Waterin' animals is a lot more pleasant task than shovelin' chicken droppin's. Pa had it so the sides of the coop could be propped open, an' you could reach in, with a short handled broad hoe an' scrape that stink out of the coop. The smell was some of the worst stink I knew of. But a pail of those chicken droppin's would make a garden grow green. I thought that this proved God had a sense of humor, an' the sayin' 'chewin' your cabbage twice' had a different meanin' ta me fer years.

"I didn't see no snake," Billy said, speculatin' I might be tellin' a fib.

"Makes no never mind ta me, I was just tryin' ta be helpful," I replied.

Billy warily approached the trough ta dip another bucket full of water, keepin' a watchful eye fer any slithery movement.

"Here," he said as he tossed the bucket in my direction. "I'll clean the stinkin' coops."

'He makes this too easy sometimes,' I thought.

Pa an' Mel came into view as the wagon rolled down the road with a small dust cloud trailin' behind. We ran across the field ta greet 'em.

"Hey, Pa! Hey, Mr. Mel! How was the trip ta town?"

"It couldn't have been better, unless we stopped fer pie," Mel said.

"Did you two git your chores done?"

"Yes sir, Pa. I cleaned out the coop real good!" Billy said makin' sure he'd git the credit.

"Whoa," Pa stopped Blue on the road. "Come on

up here boy."

Pa reached down an' lifted little Bill up ta the seat. Pa scooted over an' handed the reins ta Billy.

"Take us home, boy," Pa said.

I ran home as straight as the crow flies. "Momma, Momma, come see!" I yelled. "Momma, Momma! Billy's drivin' the wagon!"

Momma heard the commotion an' came out on the porch. She saw her youngest bringin' home the wagon, drivin' it like a man. Billy sat a little hutched over, kinda relaxed like. He looked like a little version of Pa. Billy directed Blue down the trail on our property that led ta the barn an' brought him ta a halt near the barn where Pa usually did.

"Good job, boy," Pa said.

"Thanks fer the ride, sir," Mel smiled as he jumped down from the wagon.

Billy was all smiles as he climbed down. He had held the reins, an' had brought the wagon home. He was right proud.

"Do you need ta go any where else, Pa?" Billy asked." "I could drive you if'n you want."

"I'm not goin' any where else today, but you can come help me put away this rig."

Unbeknownst ta me, Mr. Johnson had come down that day with his tractor an' bushhog an' cleared out a big section of land where the men were gonna build the pigpens an' barn. He also turned up the soil ta give it a solid base. It didn't take long. The pens were goin' up fast. They was gonna tack up a heavy chicken wire on the lower portion of the fence so that the hogs couldn't root out, an' make it harder fer fox, gators, an' such ta git in.

The plan was ta grow those cute little pigs into fat hogs in as short as time as possible an' sell 'em into the market, an' make some money. Uncle Joe had a season or more of feed corn stored ta fatten up the pigs. Mel was gonna construct a pump ta bring up water from the pond ta hold in a reservoir as a convenience, so no one would have to haul it. I also heard him tellin' Pa 'bout runnin some kinda water system ta each pen, so's that all the pig troughs could be filled just by openin' a spicket. Pa had never heard of such an idea'r. Mel thought he could fasten some metal or wooden-type gutters ta the rails of the pens. Once the reservoir was opened, gravity would allow the water ta flow through the twisted maze of gutters an' empty inta separate troughs, waterin' the pigs with little work. More important he had noticed Mr. Moyer had a pile of old gutters back behind his barn. So this might be constructed fer little more than time an' sweat. Uncle Joe had told Mel ta see what it would take ta put it all together, an' what Mr. Moyer wanted fer the gutters. Pa had bought a lot of fence posts fer the pens, an' Mel found himself out in the woods cuttin' saplin's down ta make the rest of the fence.

Mel spent all of his time that week over on the Prichert property. He really had a method ta what he was doin'. He was buildin' gates that would slide up an' down. The way he fashioned the pens was pretty clever. He made the fence panels slidin' in or out so that the pens could git bigger or smaller. Pa an' Uncle Joe at first didn't seem too pleased, cause they never did it this way before. Once Mel gave 'em a demonstration on how they could quickly separate sick pigs from a pen, momma an' baby pigs, an' hogs goin' ta market, just by dividin' 'em out by slidin' in a fence panel, they was impressed.

Pa an' Uncle Joe would work an' hoe the field's daily, do some irrigatin' an' such. They had ta keep up with all the routine chores 'round the farm, then they'd go over, an' help Mel at Prichert's. They was workin' from early mornin' ta dark every day. They claimed Mel was gettin' the work done of three men. Mr. Moyer ended up given Mel the gutters, he had no use fer 'em an' said if Pa could use 'em, he was welcome ta 'em. Mel hauled 'em away, an' with strips of chicken wire an' tar, constructed a waterin' system that saved Billy an' me a lot of water haulin' fer sure. Mr. Moyer even came over ta see what Mel was up ta. He was dumbfounded as ta Mel's creativity.

"Either you're one of the smartest men I ever met,

or you're the laziest! This contraption will save a body a lot of luggin'."

Pa was real grateful ta Mr. Moyer fer the gutters. Momma sent him home with biscuits an' some of her homemade jam. She also invited him ta Sunday dinner. That Saturday, Pa an' Uncle Joe was brin'in' their hogs over ta their newly built pens. Now mind you, these pens were but a stone's throw across the road from our house, but I could clearly hear that gruntin' an' squealin', as if they were still just outside my window. Pa an' Mel had been given the ponds a walk 'round every day with their shotguns. They never was able ta git an eye on that gator. There was signs of places he'd come out of the water, but we hadn't seen that old log floatin' on the water.

Uncle Joe got a hold of some old wire cable an' fashioned some snares, like the kind you'd make fer catchin' rabbits. The only difference was instead of lookin' like little lassos; it looked like he was goin' ta hang a person. Uncle Joe set three snares on the paths it seemed the gator used the most. These snares were set directly on the path so that when the gator would crawl ta the bait set out, the gator's head would go through the loop; the more the gator tried ta shake of the wire, the more it would cinch down.

Uncle Joe had the wire fastened ta some heavy rope an' that was tied ta a nearby tree. If'n that gator's head went through that snare, Uncle Joe would be skinnin' him, an' eatin' him fer sure. Now, gator wasn't a part of his normal diet, but Uncle Joe had hunted an' fished all his life. He'd rather eat somethin' he caught or killed than somethin' he paid fer. It's not he was a skinflint; his feelin's were "that's just the way it oughtta be."

I don't even know if'n it was legal ta hunt gators. But a man can do what he needs ta or wants ta on his land. Except makin' moonshine... unless it's fer personal use. These are the things children hear men say when they think we're not listenin'. Pa an' Uncle Joe were real happy at everythin' gittin' done that week. Uncle Joe figured they had close ta ninety pigs an' hogs. They should buy a dozen or so feeder pigs ta fill out their stock.

They had plenty of room with their new pens fer growth; an' should hang out their shingle as ta bein' in the hog trade. Pa agreed, an' that was the beginnin' of the Gilbert Hog Co. Pa's hog, Oscar, an' Uncle Joe's hog, Puddin' Head, would be their breeders. Both Uncle Joe an' Pa had been offered good money fer them hogs, but they'd never let 'em go. Uncle Joe said they was worth their weight in gold an' tasted twice as good. Mel had a bit of tweakin' ta do at the Prichert's. He was feedin' the hogs in the mornin' as well as puttin' together a grain bin Uncle Joe had brought over from his property ta store the feed in.

It was gittin' on ta mid-afternoon that Saturday, I was in the back with Billy. We was catchin' bees in a jar. Billy wanted ta start a hive so's he could get honey anytime he wanted. We knew bees made honey; we just weren't so sure on how ta get 'em ta build a hive. Now, I hear Mel; he's out in front of the house hollerin'. I got no idea'r what he was so excited 'bout, but it wasn't in his nature ta be so loud. Pa came out of the barn lookin' fer Billy an' me. I was thinkin' he thought Mel was yellin' 'bout one of us. He kinda half run ta the front of the house with little Bill, a jar of bees, an' me in tow.

"Joe caught himself a big gator! He's thrashin' all over! You'd better git him an' your shotguns over ta the far pond quick! I don't know if that snare will hold."

"You two stay right here," Pa said as he ran in ta the house. He came out as quick as he went in, shotgun in hand. He yelled ta us.

"You two run over ta Uncle Joe's, tell 'em ta bring his skinnin' knife. He's got a gator ta gut. Now you two stick together, an' don't dally on the way! Catch a ride with him back here. Go on now, git goin'," He instructed. We ran through the cotton fields as fast as our little legs would move. We cut through a stand of trees an' across a road. We caught our breath a minute an' started through Uncle Joe's field's.

"I wonder how big it is?" Billy wondered. "I want one of his claws an' one of his teeth," he said as he jumped row after row of young cotton plants.

Uncle Joe saw us comin' before we saw him. He had already started hitchin' up his wagon an' had his rifle, knife an' saw in the wagon's bed.

"Uncle Joe, you caught the gator! Pa said, come quick! Mr. Mel said

it's tearin' up the countryside, an' the tree that the rope's 'round is nearly

pulled up by the roots!" Billy blurted out.

Uncle Joe looked at the third eye in Billy's forehead. "Boy, that tree is a good twenty-two inches 'round. If that gator's rippin' it out by the roots, it'd be so big we could see it from here!"

"Now, you two stay away from my gun," he told us. "Billy, you can sit up front with me."

"Papa," Janey said as she come runnin' up ta the wagon, "we want ta go, too!"

"We're all goin'," Aunt Lee said as she came out the front screen door with Dorothy.

"I've heard 'bout this gator fer years; now I'm gonna see it! Billy, you can sit up here 'tween your Uncle an' me. You girls git in the back an' stay away from Papa's rifle."

That ride ta our house seemed to take forever. Momma was standin' on the road in front of our house as we rode up.

"Killin' an old gator is turnin' out ta be a family gatherin'," Momma smiled.

"I haven't heard any shots; Mel said it's on the far pond," Momma told Uncle Joe.

"All right, y'all can come, but keep them, children, back, unless I says otherwise," Uncle Joe instructed.

We went across the road. Momma held Billy's hand so he wouldn't dart ahead an' wind up down a gator's throat. As we come up ta the second pond Mel an' Pa were standin' off a bit, at the head of the pond. Uncle Joe was movin' up on the creature as it laid in the tall grass by the water's edge. The rope Uncle Joe had used with the snare wouldn't reach the pond, an' was holdin' fast. He didn't want the gator ta get back in the water once it was caught.

"He's been askin' fer you, Joe," Mel said with an elfin grin.

"Yeah, Joe, he's gotta bone ta pick with you 'bout leavin' wire's layin' 'round an' such," Pa added.

Uncle Joe paid no never mind ta what they was sayin'. He was fixed on the gator's mouth, on account o' there were a lot of teeth in that mouth. The gator slung his head to an' fro the nearer Uncle Joe got. It made a hissin' sound an' snapped his jaws a time or two. The tall grass hadn't been bush hogged down like the other pond. That gator had flattened it all where he was by rollin' over an' over again an' again tryin' ta get loose. The wire had cut into his neck, rubbin' it raw. As Uncle Joe drew up close, the gator jerked away then started a kinda rollin' dance I'll never fergit. It started rollin' right at Uncle Joe.

"Joe, git out of the way!" Pa shouted.

As quick as lightnin', Uncle Joe jumped straight up as the gator rolled under him. Its tail gave Uncle Joe's leg a whack! He went head over heels. His rifle went towards the pond, an' so did he. He landed on his back, not knowin' where he was, an' what's worst, where was the gator. Pa rushed ta help Uncle Joe up. Mel ran over by the tree ta take up slack on the rope so's the gator couldn't reach 'em. It looked like Mel was walkin' his gator on a leash.

Aunt Lee had a look that said, "If that gator don't bite you, Joe T. I will!"

Uncle Joe was mad when he got up. He grabbed his gun, walked up ta the gator, put his gun 'tween his eyes an' BANG! That gator rolled a bit more, quivered a moment, an' then went limp.

"I won't be messin' 'round with you all afternoon," Uncle Joe said, an' gave himself the once over checkin' fer scrapes an' bumps.

Mel walked up ta the gator an' kicked its tail a little. There was no response. There was a tad of blood dribblin' down from 'tween the gator's eyes. Pa grabbed him by the tail an' back leg an' started ta roll 'im on his back. Mel gave him a hand.

"This thin' is over ten foot long." Mel said. "He could have easily ate a child or two who'd a sneaked down ta his pond." He looked over at Billy with a smile.

"I'd have never come here without my Pa," Billy said. "Can I touch him?"

"If you want ta touch him come on over; he won't bite now," Pa offered.

All of us children edged over ta the beast an' felt its scaly tough hide. Billy inspected its claws an' teeth.

"Can I have a claw an' some of its teeth?" Billy asked.

"I don't want parts of that critter floatin' 'round my house!" Momma answered.

"I'd keep it in my special box, Momma," Billy promised.

Momma thought a moment. "Child, what do you have in that box right now?"

"Just stuff... my stuff," Billy answered, thinkin' 'bout what Momma would find if she opened that box.

We crawled 'round that carcass like ants at a picnic. It's not often you git ta study a creature such as this up close. Even Momma an' Aunt Lee got a good look. They didn't touch it or nothin'; they just kinda looked at it with a pained gaze. We had once been down ta south-central Louisiana, down by the Atchafalaya Basin. There must be a million acres of swamp an' gators, snakes, an' all sorts of creepy-crawly critters. We saw live gators, skinned gators, even barbecued gators, but this gator; he was ours. It musta made its way through creeks an' marshland from the Choctaw slough over ta the west. It made its home here, an' now it looked like Billy's special box would be its new home, at least fer parts of him.

"Ok, let's go," Momma said. "I've seen all I care too."

"I'm with you, Annie," Aunt Lee said as she turned on her heel ta leave.

"Pa, can we stay an' watch you skin 'em?" Billy asked.

"Pleeeeeease!" The length of time it took him ta git that one word out of his throat coulda allowed someone else the time ta recite the Lord's Prayer.

"If they want ta stay, they can. You children just stay back an' watch."

Janey an' Dorothy went with Momma an' Aunt Lee, Billy an' me stayed behind. Mel just stood there lookin' on.

"I don't know of what help I can be. I've cleaned a fish or two an' plucked a couple of chickens, but I've never dressed out anythin' this big."

"Joe's gutted deer, bear, most thin's that walk on all fours 'round here. This is his deal," Pa said as he stepped back himself. Uncle Joe went straight ta work.

"You know I've eat gator before. It's pretty good," Uncle Joe commented, never lookin' up from the task at hand.

"What does it taste like?" Billy asked.

"It reminds me of chicken when its barbecued out doors," he grunted as he sliced through the leathery skin.

"Can I feed the innards ta the hogs?" Billy asked. "They'll eat anythin'."

"Boy," was all Pa could git out.

"No!" Uncle Joe said as he stopped an' looked at little Bill.

"If you was ta feed those gator innards ta the hogs, they'd end up growin' teeth like a gator! You'd get too close to 'em at feedin' time, an' SNAP!!! Them hogs would eat you alive, boy," Uncle Joe was spinnin' a tall one ta Billy. Billy just stood there, stone face, lookin' into the eyes of Mel an' Pa ta tell him it ain't so.

"Joe, don't be tellin' the boy tales like that," Pa said.

"Otis, you tellin' me you don't 'member the gator pigs we saw as kids on the Henry's farm?" Uncle Joe would never give up.

"No, I don't, but I 'member that mule that kicked you in the head. Maybe some of that jack-ass wore off on you."

Mel laughed as he held the gator's shoulders still so Uncle Joe could finish his chore. Mel got a shovel an' ended up buryin' the innards, back in the woods. Uncle Joe finished skinnin' out that gator an' went on ta tannin' the hide. Mel suggested he take the meat over ta Mr. Moyer's an'

see if he'd put it in his smoke house, which he did. Uncle Joe ended up boilin" the meat off that gator's skull an' gave it ta Billy. He kept it out in the barn fer years. Momma an' Aunt Lee wanted nothin' ta do with any of that gator meat, an' had no intention of cookin" it in any of their fry pans.

"You can put it on the grill out side if you want it cooked, an' after it's grilled I want that gr,ill scraped an' cleaned when you're done!" Momma ordered with no signs of negotiations ta be made.

I did have some of that gator, an' I'm here ta say, it did remind me of chicken. We fished those ponds countless times in my childhood. I would enjoy the many conversations my pa an' I had there. That evenin' as Billy an' I was comin' in the house fer bedtime, Mel gave us each a carved animal. Again Billy got the boy, an' I got the girl. These were long neck giraffes. Mel had carved the spotted patterns on 'em, an' big ears. Their antlers were little nubbins atop their heads. We thanked Mel. Billy told him he liked lions. That was just like Billy.

Chapter 13

The next day at church, the word came from Mr. Moyer his dog, Sally, had a litter of pups, five in all, an' in a couple of days Billy could come over an' put his dibs in on one. Mr. Moyer took supper with us. It was a pleasant time havin' him over. Pa had warned Billy ta not pester Mr. Moyer concernin" the puppy 'n all. As soon as Mr. Moyer left, little Bill was on Momma like fly on honey.

"I wonder what they look like? What should I name it? Do you think I could teach it ta be a huntin' dog?"

He had a million questions. "Can it sleep in my bed with me?"

"No!" was the one answer Pa was sure of. "That dog will live outside an' never come into this house. If it wants ta git out of the wind or rain, pray God's givin' it enough sense ta git in the barn. An' it better learn early my chickens are not ta be bothered. If'n this dog turns out ta be a bird killer, I'll take it fer a walk in the woods an' come home alone!"

The rules were set. It'd be up ta Billy ta train it, an' with Pa, there was no second chances when it came ta a chicken killer. He couldn't afford it; an' wouldn't stand fer it. On Monday, the Gilberts were the talk of the schoolyard again. One week it's little Bill gittin' bit by a copperhead; this week, it's how the Gilbert men hunted down a gator fifteen feet long, with a mouth full of six inch daggers. It was also out that this gator had eaten five of our cows, which was funny seein' how we only had four. The thin's people say when they don't know nothin' is beyond me. It seemed the bigger the fib, the easier it was fer 'em ta believe.

Billy had saved some of the left over belly skin Mel was ta bury. He had picked off the scales an' said he'd trade or sell 'em. Two scales fer a penny. That was the goin' rate, an' he only had a few. So if'n you had ta have one, you'd better pony up. The girls, Janey an' Dorothy, had ta explain why they weren't there, seein' how it was their Papa who climbed up on the back of the mighty beast an' slayed it.

We said their Ma wouldn't let 'em stay; she felt it was dangerous an' all. We told everyone how they fought an' screamed as they were drug off from the battle. But they could hear their Papa fightin' an' cussin' the creature into the pit of Hades. Not a word was doubted. We had the scales as proof, an' little Bill was considerin' a fee fer a viewin' of the monster's skull, which he kept in an old wooden crate out in the barn. These were the stories legends gave birth to. Pa was workin' the fields when we got home. Momma was in the kitchen. Mel was nowhere ta be seen. I figured he was 'round back or over ta the Prichert property.

"How was your school day? Do ya have much homework?" Momma asked. We told her how everyone wanted ta know 'bout catchin' the gator.

"How 'bout your studies, arithmetic, spellin', history?" she inquired.

Those were always fine. I thought the interestin' news would be if'n there was a fight in the schoolyard, who got in trouble with Miss Dunham, or if someone had a new pair of shoes. These were scraps of news worth tellin'. I took a piece of bread with butter an' sugar on it into the yard. I saw Mel comin' from the Prichert's. As he got closer, I got ta thinkin' that the pens were built, an' it'd be a spell before Pa was ready ta put up a barn over there, even a little one. Mel had helped with a lot of fixin' an' mendin' since he showed up. Was there gonna be enough work ta keep him busy now, or would be movin' along? I didn't want him ta go, but he was takin' no interest in any local girls. He seemed just set on helpin' Pa out fer food an' the few wages he was earnin'. An' there was that somethin' special 'bout Mel, those thin's I saw, an' thin's I didn't see.

Those times that caused me ta wonder.

"Afternoon, Mr. Mel," I greeted

"An' a good afternoon ta you, Miss Eula," He replied.

"How are you this fine day?" he asked.

"I'm pert'near good," I replied.

"Been workin' hard?" I searched out.

"So far." His brown an' green eye sparkled when he smiled.

"I'll bet there's plenty ta do with all that's goin' on over ta the Prichert's, the fields an' such. Pa said he just didn't think there was enough hours in the day."

"I'm sure we'll be doin somethin' with these pens an' shelters here," Mel said, pointin' ta the fenced-in pens Pa had been keepin' the pigs in.

"I'm sure your Ma will appreciate the new found fresh air," he smiled.

"I didn't notice the smell till it was gone," I had admitted.

"The smell makes no never mind ta me, exceptin' fer the chicken coop, NOW that's a smell that feels like a thump in the face."

I laughed, 'memberin' how I got Billy ta clean out the coop the other day.

"Well, Pumpkin, I'm gonna head out ta see if I can give your Pa a hand an' git a few more things done before supper."

An' with that, he headed across the field ta where Pa was. I wandered 'round the back of the barn, finishin' my bit of bread. I found myself lookin' in the doorway of the shed. I peeked in ta see where Mel was sleepin'. I spied his wonderful wooden box, which held all his special tools. His satchel was atop an old crate he appeared ta be usin' as a table. I could see inside if'n I stood at the right angle. Mel's clothes were folded neatly in his satchel, an' on the workbench was his little black leather drawstrin' coin purse. This is the coin purse he had kept that ten dollar gold piece in. I wondered how much money he had. Were there more gold coins? Brand new coins? I wanted ta walk over an' open that black little mystery, but how bad would that be! An' I couldn't stand the thought if I was caught.

I walked away, an' started 'round the corner of the barn. I saw Mel an' Pa a ways off walkin' towards the other end of the field. I could hear Momma talkin' ta Billy in the house. I turned an' strolled back, retracin' my steps slowly as not ta be noticed. I walked into the shed an' straight ta the coin purse. 'Memberin' exactly how it was laid down I opened it, an' found it-empty, not even the change from that ten-dollar gold piece he spent at Miss Marie's buyin' his shoes an' socks a few weeks back was in there. I pinched the leather pouch between my fingers, searchin' fer an outline of coins hidden an' unseen... nothin'. I quickly pulled the strings closed an' placed it back exactly where I found it. Didn't Pa pay him anythin' yet? Mel hadn't a cent his name. He may have kept his money somewhere else, but most people kept it in their purses or wallets. They never carried it in their pockets workin' chores. If Pa wasn't given Mel no money fer all his work, well he could up an' leave at anytime. What's the reason ta stay 'round? I never saw Pa payin' Mel no wages, but that was grown-up business, no need fer children's eyes ta witness private dealin's 'tween adults.

I felt like I did somethin wrong lookin' in Mel's coin purse an' all, an' now I was worried 'bout Mel, an' his financial situation. I was irritated with my pryin' eyes, an' the worries an' sadness they caused me over the past days. I skedaddled out of that shed in a heartbeat. Again as I rounded the corner of the barn, Pa an' Mel were still out in the field; Momma was

inside with Billy, an' I was just mean'erin' my way through the yard when off in the distance I heard what sounded like bells, different tones an' pitches minglin' together, kinda dancin' across the fields. I looked down the road, an' I saw a ways off the wagon, man! He had a collection of bells an' chimes fixed firmly ta his wagon. They announced his arrival. Now the wagon man would come 'round from time ta time. His name was Mr. Sims. He was older than Pa, with long gray tresses, an' face hair. He always wore a tie, I guess 'cause he was a businessman an' all. He pretty much had a general store loaded up in his wagon. He would sharpen knives an' scissors. He sold everythin' from sweets an' toys ta rugs an' currycombs. He was also current on news from all the surroundin' counties. He was a-rollin' newspaper of sorts. He'd deliver, notes an' letters, packages an' greetin's ta an' from families an' friends from far off. I waved Pa an' Mel in off the field. Billy's ears had caught the rin'in'. I could tell by the way he bolted from the house. Momma hollered ta me ta call Pa. We all headed ta the road in front of our house. Pa an' Mel got there just as the wagon man rolled up. Momma had prepared a pitcher of ice water fer the three men. Billy an' I were walkin' 'round Mr. Sims' wagon, lookin' at his wares packed an' strapped ta every possible hitchin' place you could imagine.

"How goes the battle, Otis?" Mr. Sims greeted Pa.

"We'll see another day, Lord willin'," Pa replied.

"Mr. Sims, this is Mel. He's come ta work here, givin' me a hand."

"Nice to meet you, sir," Mel reached out his hand ta Mr. Sims.

Mr. Sims took Mel's hand like a hen on a worm, shakin' it hard an' long.

"Where do you hail from, son?" he asked.

"From all over, mainly back east," Mel replied.

My ears perked up. Mel never shared a lot of his past, an' Mr. Sims was just the type ta find out how many teeth you have left in your mouth.

"You married, Mel? I've got some pretty things here fer the Missus," Mr. Sims started sellin'.

"No, sir. I guess I'm one of God's unclaimed blessin's."

"I guess I'm a part of that group myself," Mr. Sims chuckled.

"But Otis, you aren't. Your bride is stan'in' there, just as pretty as the day she said, 'I do'. You need to look at a few things I have so she doesn't start regrettin' those two words."

"I don't mind the lookin'. It's the buyin' I have ta watch out fer." Pa grinned.

Momma started lookin' at some fabric Mr. Sims had peekin' out of a box at the back of the wagon. Pa studied an ax handle.

"You got any licorice or rock candy?" Billy asked.

"Boy, you bet I do. I also got some chocolates from New York City. An' the best salt water taffy you'll ever taste!"

Billy's eyes got big as cup saucers. He looked at Pa, who avoided eye contact.

"Billy," Mel called. "Would you run an' git my coin purse off the work bench in the shed?"

"Sure!" Billy said, sensin' an opportunity ta share

in some sweets Mel might buy. He was off ta retrieve that coin purse I had peered into moments before.

"I'll help him," I ran off after him. Billy was comin' out of the shed as I rounded the corner.

"I'll run it back ta him," I said. "I'm faster." I took a holt of the leather pouch.

"I'm helpin' Mel!"

He snatched it away an' ran ta the front of the house where everyone was. I trailed behind. Billy handed Mel's black leather coin purse ta him. Mel thanked Billy an' put the purse in his pocket. How was Mel gonna buy anythin' with an empty purse?

"I'd be interested in a blanket, a cotton one, if your stockin' one," Mel inquired.

"I've got a great blanket. It'll keep you as warm as the wife you don't have," Mr. Sims assured Mel of his wares.

"We are also gonna need to try some of that chocolate...an' taffy."

Billy's eyes got big, an' his grin could touch both of his ears. Mr. Sims opened a box of taffy. Mel handed one ta Billy an' me. Mr. Sims climbed in his wagon ta unpack the blanket fer Mel's inspection. Billy started chewin' his taffy, drool formin' at the corner of his mouth. He made that suckin' sound as not ta lose a drop of sweetness. I couldn't unwrap my piece of pleasure. I knew Mel couldn't afferd it. I was ready ta return it when it came ta light Mel had no money. Mr. Sims emerged from the back of the wagon with a large blanket.

"That is a warm lookin' blanket, Mel," Momma said as she felt the corner of the coverlet.

Mel inspected the blanket an' wrapped it 'round himself. "How do I look?" he questioned.

"You look like your ready fer bed," Pa smiled.

"I'll take it, an' some chocolate, an' a box of that taffy."

Mel folded up the blanket an' handed it back ta Mr. Sims. Mel reached into his pocket ad pulled out his change purse. He loosened them drawstrings, openin' the mouth of the purse wide. He shook the small pouch slightly an' peeked inside. Then, reachin' in with his thumb an' forefinger, he pulled out a ten dollar gold piece. He turned his head towards me an' smiled. I couldn't believe my eyes!

"Go ahead, Pumpkin, eat your taffy. I got some chocolate for you to try, too. He paid Mr. Sims.

Pa bought an ax handle. Momma got a parin' knife; an' Pa bought her a pretty scarf. She told him, no, but he insisted. Mel put his coin purse back in his pocket. This time it was heavy with change. It had a jin'le as he dropped it in his pants. I couldn't understan' how I missed that gold piece, another bran' new coin. Mr. Sims climbed up on his wagon, thanked everyone fer their business an' jin'le-jangled away.

Momma took her scarf into the house an' put it away, turnin' her attention towards supper. Pa went an' replaced the handle on one of the axes. Billy tagged along. I saw Mel disappear with his blanket. He was probably puttin' it on his bed. I continued ta wonder how I could've missed seein' that coin. I was workin' away on a piece of taffy when I sat down at our backyard table. I started watchin' an ant, draggin' a dead bug across the tabletop. I got no idea'r where it was goin, but it was determined on gettin' there. Mel came up ta me as I sat there. Again, I thanked him fer the taffy, as I was still chewin', an' suckin' it off my teeth.

"Think nothin' of it, Pumpkin, I'm glad you're enjoyin' it. We're gonna have some chocolate fer dessert tonight, all the way from New York!"

"I wish we had chocolate plants an' taffy plants 'stead of these old cotton plants!" I dreamed out loud.

"God does provide fer us daily. Look here; today you're eatin' taffy an' chocolate!" Mel pointed out.

"Oh! I'm thankful ta you an' God. You had that shiny new gold piece, 'n all, an' God created sugar!" I explained with a giggle.

"Well, Pumpkin, you got ta understand'in everythin' I have or will ever have, comes from God. He provides all I need."

"Well, gold coins come from a bank..." I began.

Mel gently interrupted me. "All thin's come from Him, Pumpkin. God provides the work to earn the money, the body to perform the labor. God provided Jesus as our way to Him. There are countless examples in the scriptures where God provided fer his own. Elijah was fed by ravens while he hid in the Kerith Ravine. He drank from the brook, an' the birds brought him bread an' meat in the mornin' an' the evenin'. That is just one of the most amazin' ways in which He provides fer His people."

Mel's complete faith in God as our provider began ta shape my young understandin' of my lovin' Heavenly Father. My knowledge of Him would grow an' mature in the years ta come in the simple understan'in' that God loves us.

"So, God provided you with that gold coin?" I asked pointedly, almost scared of the answer.

"Yes... yes he did, Pumpkin," he slowly, an' firmly replied. "Fer I am His, an' He is mine."

Momma called me in ta help with the table. Mel gave me a pat on the head an' a piece of taffy fer later. We sat 'round the supper table that night, an' I thought of all God had given me. My family, a place ta live,

food, so much, my little heart was full. I started readin' the Bible at the kitchen table not long after that day. I figured that's where God provided the food fer my belly, that's where he could provide the food fer, my soul.

Chapter 14

The next couple of days seemed like Pa an' Mel were as busy as bees in a flower garden. We had our first fish supper from the ponds; it was a good fry. Uncle Joe brought in two dozen baby pigs. They ate an' squealed all the time. I was thankful fer the pump an' waterin' system Mel had rigged. It saved a load of work fer Billy an' me. An' it was fun watchin' the water flow through the troughs after bein' released from the reservoir. The next day Mel had a carved pair of lions an' set 'em beside each of our breakfast plates. Once again a boy lion fer Billy, an' a girl lion fer me.

"Thank-you Mr. Mel." We both said as we sat down ta breakfast.

It was gett'n ta be like Christmas every few days.

"This is just what I wanted." Billy was so happy.

Pa was just sittin' there studyin' 'em. "How do you carve 'em so quick?" Pa asked Mel over his mornin' bacon an' eggs.

"I start with smaller pieces of wood, an' I keep my

tools real sharp. I've always been able ta get through a hunk of wood pretty fast. The detail comes easy, pretty much as second nature," Mel explained.

"I declare," Momma said, "you have a great gift. That cross you carved fer Eula is so attractive, an' she has received so many compliments. I'm surprised you haven't been swamped with requests ta carve more."

"Well, I barely have time to carve the things I want to, let alone take on orders," Mel smiled. "I carve fer pleasure, an' to relax before I go to sleep. I have no intent to makin' it into a chore."

"Did you sleep well, child?" Momma asked.

"Yes, Ma'am," I replied sleepily.

"Mornin', Honey," Pa said as he stroked the back of my head.

I sat an' ate my breakfast, listenin' ta the men talk as Momma was busy cookin', bakin' an' cleanin'. They was gonna replace some sidin' on the barn, an' start pullin' down the old fence where we had kept the pigs. Pa said he could use that fencin' over at the Prichert's, an' he was thinkin' of puttin' in a crop of goobers, or maybe some kinda berry. Momma would be happy with either. Billy was up soon after I finished breakfast. He was dressed an' ready fer school. This was our last week of school before summer vacation. Billy loved summer vacation. He just had no interest in studies. I loved school, an' bein' with my friends every day, but I loved summers too! I was plannin' ta go explorin' with Janey an' Dorothy on our first day. Maybe we could even have a camp out! I'd talk ta the girls on the way ta school. We would prepare both our folks fer a camp out. We'd start hintin' now 'bout what a great time we had last year sleepin' on the wagon bed, watchin' the stars. Billy saw a shootin' star go clean across the sky.

The summer stars were so bright an' clear. I could fall asleep just admirin' their twinklin' in the dark. I got so I could point out constellations, an' not just the dippers, I could spot the arrow, when it was in season, as well as the triangle, an' the lyre. Some of the other constellations were just too hard ta tell. Even if Pa was there ta point 'em out I couldn't tell what they were.

"Eula, git little Bill an' git goin'. You're gonna run late if you don't git a move on."

Billy an' I ran out the back door. Pa an' Mel were pullin' down the fence an' stackin' it in the wagon. They waved us a good-bye, an' we were off.

"You think Pa will let me go fishin at the ponds next week?" Billy asked.

"Oh sure, he'll let you go down ta that pond alone where Uncle Joe killed that gator that could've swallowed you down in one gulp!" I was a little sarcastic ta say the least.

"There was only one!" Billy protested.

"We only saw one, an' it took pert'near a week ta see that one," I pointed out.

"I do think Pa will take you pretty regular," I conceded. "He likes fishin' there as much as you do."

Janey an' Dorothy come runnin' up, an' we walked the rest of the way ta school mappin' out our plan ta git our overnight. Half the fun of gittin' together was all the connivin' we did ta git there. At lunch we sat out in the grass an' talked of the long days of summer.

"Ya know, I heard there's an old graveyard way back in the woods over by the church. It was a Negro cemetery, an' now it's all overgrown with weeds, an' brush." Janey spoke of a possible adventure.

"I never heard of any such thin'," Billy scoffed.

"An' just how old are you?" I questioned.

"I'm nine years old, Eula Mae. Old enough ta know 'bout some lost graveyard," he defended.

"Nine years old, an' you think you've heard all there is ta hear 'round here? Well, Billy Ray, I've heard a thin' or two 'bout you. Maybe we should set 'round here an' talk 'bout 'em 'stead of the graveyard?" That shut him up. He just set there eatin' on the meat an' biscuit Momma had give us fer lunch.

"I heard there are old bones lyin' right on top of

the ground. Some of 'em graves go back a hundred years or more. Who knows what we might find?" Janey said.

"I don't think we should be goin' into a graveyard, an' disturbin' the dead." Dorothy said, a bit uneasy.

"They may come an' haunt you if'n you do, but don't worry 'bout what I say, I'm just a little kid," Billy said with biscuit crumbs fallen off his chin.

"I say we don't be tellin' anyone else 'bout it, an' first chance we git, we go explorin'!" I was sure they'd all follow.

Now this was what summers were made of, the unknown, somethin' different, a change from the ordinary. We always had fishin' an' swimmin'.

We had the sun in the day, an' the stars, an' moon at night. An' now we had a graveyard an' all the mysteries that would brin'. This is what our young lives needed, somethin' ta look ferward ta. The afternoon slipped away into a chasm of lost an' forgotten afternoons. We came home ta see Pa an' Mel had changed the look of our backyard. There was no longer a fenced-in corral fer pigs, an' the cows. It was now wide open. The chicken coop still stood next ta the barn, an' the barbed wire fence off in the back was as far as the cows could go now. No longer did they have free range up close ta the house. They'd come in the barn from the rear access. I liked it; it opened up our property. A crop of blackberries back there would be nice, some green where all that mud an' smell had been. Mel was bangin' nails into the side of the barn. Pa was handin' him panels an' helpin' hold 'em in place. Little Bill an' I waved hi an' went in an' sat with Momma.

"Hey, ta you two. What kinda homework ya'll got tonight?" Momma asked.

"None fer me." Billy replied.

"I just gotta practice my spell'n words." I said.

"How do you like the backyard, Momma?" I asked.

"I like it a lot, Sweet Pea. I think it will smell better than it did last summer. 'specially when that swelterin' heat an' humidity comes on us," Momma said with a smile.

"I will like havin' a yard full of berries. Pies, muffins, cobblers, an' preserves, we'll have our work cut out fer us at the end of the season," she added.

"You'll be cannin' an' puttin' up preserves. Your fin'ers will be stained with that blackberry juice fer weeks," Momma warned.

"I don't give a lick 'bout that, just as long as we have the berries," I assured Momma I would be happy ta help.

Momma asked Billy an' me ta take some water out ta Pa an' Mel. They'd been workin' hard.

"How you two likin' this new yard here?" Pa

asked as he put the glass ta his lips.

"I like it a lot!" Billy answered. "I like that there's gonna be black berries in the yard' stead of pigs an' cows."

"Now, who said anythin' 'bout berries?" Pa questioned.

"Momma said we was gonna have berry bushes an' her an' Eula was gonna made lots of pies an' cobblers." Billy could almost taste the berries bustin' open in his mouth.

"Oh well, if'n your Momma put her claim in on berries, I guess we gotta make her happy," Pa resigned, with a wink at Mel.

"I was thinkin' a peanut patch..." Pa started.

Now Billy loved boiled goobers, an' he loved black berry pie, so Pa had put him in a quan'ary.

"Couldn't we grow both?" Billy asked.

"Maybe. I don't know if'n there'd be enough room," Pa answered.

"We'll just let your Momma decided," Pa concluded.

"I love berries, juicy an sweet," Mel said as he put his empty glass down.

"You know, I saw quite a few berry bushes out in the woods over at the Prichert's property. They looked real healthy. We might be able ta dig 'em up an' replant 'em here," Mel thought out loud.

"You two check with your Momma on what she's

leanin' ta an' that's what we're doin...tell her I hopes it's berries. Let me an' Mel finish up this barn." Pa scooted us out of there so's they could finish. We took their empty glasses in an' did some of the last homework we'd be doin' fer awhile. Billy talked 'bout gettin'' his dog in a few weeks, as soon as it was weaned. He still wasn't certain as ta which pup he'd pick. He didn't want the runt, but he was afraid no one else would take him, an' the thought of an unloved pup was more than his little heart could bear. He didn't say it, but I knew it was so. The next couple of days were uneventful, in the eyes of a child. We were finishin' up our school days. Pa an' Mel were runnin' the farm, day-ta-day maintenance, improvements, an' the expansion of our little farm was on their backs. I was glad Pa had Mel. Pa seemed happier workin' day in an' day out with him. It just made his load lighter. All the things he wanted ta do were gettin done. The farm was in the best shape ever.

When we got up fer breakfast Friday mornin', Momma was makin' flapjacks an' bacon. This was Billy's an' my best breakfast, an' Momma was makin' it special fer us on our last day of school. Pa an' Mel were happy it was our last day of school; they enjoyed the meal too. Pa was gonna be happy ta have our "legs" ta do some of his fetchin' of this an' that. We were his little mules in the summer when we weren't off swimmin' an' explorin'. We met up with Janey an' Dorothy as well as a few others. We was all excited at it bein' our last day of school.

"Papa said he was gonna buy us a pony this summer," Dorothy said.

"A pony?" Billy asked. "Can I ride 'im?"

"Sure," Dorothy started.

"But you'll have ta take turns shovelin' out his stall," Janey negotiated.

"You bet if I can ride him all by myself," Billy said, tryin' ta seal the deal.

Boy oh, oh boy, what a summer we were gonna have. We got ta school an' Miss Dunham had us turn in our books an' clean out our desks. Then we washed our desks top ta bottom. We each had assignments; cleanin' the chalkboard, sweepin' the floor, stackin' the books in the bookcase. Some of the children had ta go out an' clean up the schoolyard. When we were all done an' the schoolhouse was squeaky clean, Miss Dunham gave us a lunch party outside. We had san'wiches an' lemonade; there was cake an' ice cream! It was a wonderful time. I'm sure if we had lunch times like that everyday Billy would go ta school ferever. We said our summer good byes an' made plans ta get together over the long months ahead.

As we walked home after our lunch, Billy hit every tree we passed with a rock. Dorothy was thinkin' up names fer the pony. Janey an' I, we was plannin' our adventure ta the graveyard. We got home early in the afternoon. Momma met us out in front of the house. We presented our report cards. I was a good student, E's, excellent an' G's fer good, Billy got G's, F's, fair an' one U, unsatsifactory.

"You'll be workin' in that field next ta your Pa 'fere your thirteen, Billy Ray,"

Momma warned him. She would sit an' work his spellin' an' 'rithmetic with him. It never seemed ta help. Momma had warm biscuits an' honey fer us. We sat 'round the table out side. Pa an' Mel joined us as we told of our lunch an' mornin' chores at school. Mel disappeared fer a moment; an' then returned with two more pairs of animals, two elephants with mighty trunks an' one with long tusks, that one was Billy's. An' two foxes, they were beautiful.

"Where are you two keepin' your animals?" Pa questioned.

"On my dresser," Billy quickly answered.

"Me too, Pa."

"You need ta keep 'em up there, so they don't get under foot," Pa instructed.

I was thinkin' Pa was pretty worried 'bout these carvin's. I don't think he ever wanted us ta play with 'em. These were "sittin' on the shelf pretties" an' not fer havin' fun with.

"Well, what are you goin' ta do with the rest of

your day?" Momma asked Billy an' me.

"Well, I thought of maybe goin' fishin'." Billy was fishin' fer an adult ta take him ta the ponds.

"Boy, I'll be sayin' this now fer yours an' your sister's ears. Don't either of you go ta the pond without an adult," Pa cast the rule in stone "No, Pa, I wasn't! I just was seein' if someone wanted ta go."

Billy was hopin' his bobber would be jerked under.

"When we're finished with this last side of the barn, I'll take you over," Pa said.

"You git the poles ready an' dig some worms," Pa told Billy.

"Okay!" Billy jumped up an' ran fer a shovel.

"If'n fishin' was a subject at school, that boy'd git a E," Momma chuckled.

"Well, Eula, what'll you be doin?" Momma asked.

"I'm not sure, I was thinkin' of goin' over an' playin' with the girls," I
replied.

That was how I celebrated the end of another school year. Runnin' with Janey an' Dorothy through the cotton fields of my youth, playin' tag.

"It's funny how life can change so quickly. How in moments it can be altered so, an' that the ripplin' effects seems ta go on forever. In one moment, you can take a deep full breath, an' in the next, there is no air ta fill your lungs. Your mind gasps fer life, the life you knew, the life that was yours.

Your vision is blurred by an unfamiliar future, one unplanned, unwanted, even undeserved," the old woman thought aloud, seemin'ly unaware of her "boy's" presence.

Chapter 15

We woke ta the rooster's crowin' like every mornin'. It was Saturday. Pa, Mel an' Uncle Joe were goin' into town ta pick up some supplies an' conduct some business. Momma was workin' on a pie an' some biscuits ta be dropped off at Mr. Moyer's. Uncle Joe brought his family over ta spend the day. Momma an' Aunt Lee were ta be workin' on some mendin' together while us children would play. It was ta be a wonderful time. Uncle Joe was ta load up a few hogs they had sold; this would be the first of their stock ta take ta market.

Mel asked if there was any children who had a taste fer rock candy. There was, of course, five hands in the air; Billy had both of his flyin' high. The men headed off, an' we children went back behind the barn, ta our little stan' of woods. Billy wanted ta play war; the girls an' I wanted ta race sticks down the creek. Billy was at the top of the ravine throwin' stones he found off in every direction. We was jumpin' over an' in the creek, as our sticks weaved back an' through the watery course.

"Eula, Eula come quick," Billy called down from the top of the ravine.

He wasn't loud in his request, an' he was a lookin' at somethin' on the other side of the rift. Me an' the girls climbed the side of the rise, grabbin' onto bushes an' clumps of grass as we hoisted ourselves ta the top. Billy motioned us ta approach quietly. We crept ferward stretchin' our necks an' strainin' our eyes ta catch a glimpse of what had Billy's full interest. There, on the other side of the knoll, was a deer, a Momma deer layin' down in some deep grass. It seemed the deer was aware of our bein' there, but it made no move ta run off. The deer seemed pretty round just layin' there an' just as I was 'bout ta open my mouth, Dorothy whispered.

"She's havin' a baby!"

"Shhh," Billy hushed.

We all just laid there as God's nature unfolded. We witnessed the birth of a fawn. We had seen kittens, an' pigs, calves, an' even chicks push an' peck their way into the world. But here, today, we saw one of God's creature's battlin' it's way from its momma belly ta the soft sweetness of God's green grass. We watched without a word spoke among us. We saw the care the mother had fer the newborn. After a time, we saw the fawn wobble to a standin' position an' trail off behind it's mother ta learn of the thin's of this new world. Once the two were out of sight, Billy flipped from his belly ta his back.

"I hope nothin' gits that little fawn. It can't move that quick."

"It'll be fine," Janey said, "Its Momma will take care of it."

"They'll probably go over ta where the creek bends into those trees an' brush an' get a drink."

"That would be a good place ta rest an' hide till the fawn gets stronger," Dorothy offered.

"Should we go check on it?" Billy asked.

"No, we need ta leave it alone, an' not bother it," I told him.

I was sure if it was up ta Billy, we'd be followin' that fawn all summer. He was a funny soul. One minute he'd be wantin' ta shoot somethin, an' the next, he'd be wantin' ta feed it. I guess a good hunter knows there is a cost, a sacrifice of life when a platter's full of meat. Through the trees, we could see a dust cloud bein' raised off in the distance. It was a wagon headed down our road. Billy wanted ta go an' see where the Momma deer had given birth; the girls an' me had no interest in that. We wanted ta go back ta racin' our sticks. Dorothy had a good one, which had already won two races. Just as another race started, an' we was dancin' in 'bout the creek, a loud shrill whistle pierced the woods.

"That's Papa," Dorothy said as she grabbed her

stick from the water an' raced from the woods.

She had dillydallied once too often when her Pa had whistled. Janey, Billy, an' I were on her heels. As we rounded the barn, I saw Momma sittin' at the table in the yard; Aunt Lee was holdin' onto her. Uncle Joe was stan'in' off a bit; Mel was by his side. Mel had his hand on Uncle Joe's shoulder. I could feel in the pit of my stomach somethin' was wrong, very wrong.

As we neared, I could hear Momma cryin'. I could see tears in everyone's eyes.

"Where's Pa?" I cried out. "Where's Pa?"

Momma stood up an' came ta Billy an' me. Billy was scared an' confused as she gathered us up in her arms.

"There was a accident at the mill when Pa was pickin' up supplies. Your Pa was hit in the head with a barrel, children. Your pa is dead children . . . our pa is dead," she told us.

I'll never forget my mother's scent. Billy an' I buried our faces into her, never wishin' ta see the light o'day again. Our world was collapsin'. Our little hearts broke as her words echoed in our ears. We felt her shake with pain as Aunt Lee scooped us all up an' helped us ta the table. I couldn't brin' myself ta peek out from my mother's blouse; I couldn't bear ta look into the eyes of my loved ones, confirmin' my mother's words. I could hear

Uncle Joe sniffin' back his tears. I could feel Janey an' Dorothy puttin' their hands on our backs. This just couldn't be true; there had ta be a mistake. I peeked out at Uncle Joe; he was wipin' his eyes with a handkerchief; Mel looked at me sadly. I buried my face into Momma's blouse again, cryin' till no sound would come. Little Bill was the first ta stand alone. I continued ta cling ta Momma.

"We need ta go bring him home," he sniffed. "We can't leave him alone in town."

Aunt Lee knelt next ta him. Takin' him into her arms, she kissed Billy's ferehead an' hugged him tightly. Momma pulled 'em both close ta us an' sobbed. Billy was actin' like Pa's little man. Uncle Joe an' Mel come over an' helped us all up.

"Billy's right," Uncle Joe said. "We need to go bring Otis home."

Aunt Lee pumped some water on a hankie an' wiped down all of our faces.

Mel helped Momma an' Aunt Lee up into the wagon. The girls, Billy, Mel, an' I sat in the back. This was the longest ride ta town I' membered. Aunt Lee sat with her arm 'round Momma the whole way. Mel sat 'tween Billy an' me, his arms 'round us. I could tell he was prayin' off an' on. I wanted nothin' ta do with a God who would take my Pa. I looked up at Mel. He was prayin'. I could see his mouth movin' ta the words. When he opened his eyes, he saw I was lookin' up at him. He smiled at me.

"Trust in God, Pumpkin. Trust in Him."

We bumped along that road. Nothin' looked familiar. The birds didn't even sin', the wind didn't blow, everythin' felt dead. A cloud covered the sun; darkness filled my heart with every turn the wagon wheel made. The closer we got ta town, the closer ta the truth we were of our Pa bein' dead. I thought if somehow we could just stay away from where his body lay, the more alive he'd be. It's funny how the mind of a child works. As we entered the town, I felt as if all eyes were on us, as if we had somethin that was catchin', like a cold or TB.

There were no familiar waves an' smiles like times before when we would come into town. Only a few nods, an' a woman or two wipin' tears from their eyes. We stopped in front of Doc Horne's place. Mel got out an' helped Momma down. Uncle Joe helped Aunt Lee.

"You children stay here till we git back," Uncle Joe said as he an' Aunt Lee helped Momma inside.

Mel stood on the front stoop. They all reemerged almost as soon as they went in.

"They haven't even bought him down here yet! The Doc hasn't made it into town yet!" Uncle Joe yelled at Mel, not that he was mad at him.

I guess some folks told Mel an' Uncle Joe they would take care of Pa an' git him ta the doctor's ta be cleaned up an' all so we could pick him up.

"Take us ta the mill," Momma requested. Tears were wellin' up.

"Annie, let 'em clean him up, please, he was hit in the head. You ought not see him like that," Uncle Joe pleaded.

"He's my husband, Joe. Take me to him," Was Momma's reply.

We all got out of the wagon an' started down the way ta the mill. Folks would stop Momma an' give her a hug, maybe pat us on the heads. As we got down toward the end of town where the mill was, there were a group of folks outside, kinda holden a vigil, out front of the mill. When we got ta the entrance, everyone sorta backed away; Uncle Johnny was there an' Mr. Roy an' Mr. Homer, as well as their wives. Pastor Blanchard got there the same time as us. There was so many folks from church. They was all greetin' Momma an' us. The closer we got ta the door, the thinner the crowd grew.

"Joe, Doc hasn't got here yet. That's why we haven't moved him,"

Mr. White said. He owned the mill. I peered inside those big slidin' barn doors. Inside was a bench. I could see my Pa's work boots peekin' out from a burlap sack that covered most of his body. I could see a puddle of dark red, almost brown blood on the ground beneath where his head was. I was sickened ta the point of faintin'. Billy put his arm 'round me.

"I want ta be with him," Momma said quietly. "Lee, tend ta my children."

Uncle Joe stepped up an' took one arm. Mel took her other. They led her into where there should be men workin' an' movin' 'bout, but all that was replaced with a silence, a respect, a fear. As I watched 'em git closer ta Pa's body. I could hear Momma's sobbin' an' could see Uncle Joe an' Mel supportin' more an' more of her weight. Uncle Joe pulled back the sack, an' Momma's sobs turned into weepin'. Momma an' Mel knelt beside Pa. Uncle Joe stooped as he continued ta hold Momma's arm.

"Dear Jesus, make it not so. Give us back our Pa." I prayed.

It looked like Mel was prayin', too. I saw him place his hand on Pa's leg an' bow his head. He seemed ta shudder. I held tight ta Billy, an' Aunt Lee squeezed us both. Then there seemed ta be somethin' goin' on. Uncle Joe come runnin' out.

"Where's the Doc? Has he got ta town yet? Find Doc Horne an' tell him ta hurry. Otis is still alive. I need some men ta help carry him down ta the Doc's office."

How could he be dead an' then not dead? How could these adults leave my Pa fer dead, just layin' on a bench fer all this time? I could see Momma restin' her head on his chest, I didn't know if she was just bein close ta him or listenin' fer a heartbeat. Aunt Lee moved us ta the side as some of the men went in ta help move Pa. I heard a group of men behind us say how Pa's skull had been crushed, an' they could hardly believe he was still breathin'.

"Why he's been laid out there fer over two hours," someone whispered.

"Otis Gilbert is the toughest man in the county!" Billy shouted back at the crowd.

Aunt Lee patted him on the shoulder an' peered back at the men ta keep quiet. A group of men slowly carried Pa ta the doctor's office on the bench. Momma followed close behind. I could see Pa's hair matted down with blood; again, I was sickened with fear fer him. Uncle Joe an' Pastor Blanchard now assisted Momma. Mel come up an' stood next ta us.

"Lee, why don't you go be with Annie? I'll watch these young'uns."

Mel took all four of us off, away from the crowd ta the other side of the street. We were stan'in' in front of Mildred's.

"Let's go in an' git y'all somethin' ta eat," Mel said.

"I'm not hungry," Billy said.

"We need ta get some food fer your Momma an' your folks," Mel said, pointin' ta Janey an' Dorothy.

"This will be a long afternoon an' night. Everyone's gonna need some nourishment," Mel advised.

We went into the boardin' house. Mel ordered lots of food ta eat there an' ta take over ta where Momma, Uncle Joe, an' Aunt Lee were. The people at Mildred's were so kind. They bought out beefsteaks, ham, an' chicken. There was potatoes, an' beans, okra an' peas an' every kinda pie you can imagine. They even had sodie pop. Aunt Lee came over ta check on us. She saw Mel had everythin' in hand. She had a bite with us; an' took some over ta Momma. I heard her tell Mel the Doc had gotten there, an' couldn't believe Pa was alive.

"It was by the grace of God," he said.

We was there till after suppertime. Mildred, the owner of the boardin' house, let us wait in the sittin' room. It was a long wait. The sun started castin' long shadows, an' Momma come in where we were. Billy an' I ran up ta her. We hugged.

"Children, Mel's gonna take you all back ta Aunt Lee's. You're gonna spend the night with the girl's. I'm gonna stay here with Pa in case he wakes up."

"I want ta stay with you, Momma," Billy cried.

"I know, Darlin', but it's best fer you ta do as you're told an' make Pa proud.

I'll see you tomorrow, we gotta pray fer your Pa, he's been hurt awful bad." Momma held us close an' said a few words ta God.

"Dear Jesus, we ask you ta hold Otis close ta you.

We ask you ta heal him an' ta give him back ta us."
That was all she could git out.

I was numb on the road ta Aunt Lee's. The day had passed like a clock with no hands. Aunt Lee let us sleep outside in the wagon. We laid there lookin' at the stars in silence, ne'er a word was spoke. I was too tired ta talk or think. I could hardly breathe on my own. Billy snuggled close. I prayed ta the God who let my Pa get hurt. I was afraid of Him. I was afraid if'n he knew how mad I was he'd up an' kill my Pa ta teach me a lesson. I was afraid if I didn't pray, he'd kill him cause I didn't pray ta Him. I didn't know what ta pray or what ta think.

"Hey y'all, you asleep yet?" It was Mel. He was at the wagon's edge.

"I wanted ta say good night. It's been a long day, an' you need ta git your rest. I was wonderin' if I could pray fer you?" He asked.

'It'd be better if'n Mel prays than me,' I thought.
"It's okay."

"Pray fer our Pa, not fer us," Billy asked quietly.
"I surely will," Mel smiled.

"Our Lord an' our Father, the Creator of the heavens above us, we come before you with a deep pain in our hearts. Today, Otis Gilbert, husban' of your servant Annie, an' father of Billy an' Eula, met with a terrible accident. You know all of this; you know his life is in your hands an' that he has one foot in your presence. We ask that you restore him completely to his family; we ask that you give 'em the strength to nurse him back to health. We thank you that you saw fit today to protect him from the call of death. We ask that his healin' comes swift an' miraculous as a testimony to your power an' goodness. Be with these young'uns; give 'em an' Annie a peaceful rest tonight. We ask you these thin's in the name of your livin' Son, an' accordin' to thy will, Amen. I recited each word Mel had spoke to help God hear the words.

Mel patted us on the heads an' said good night. I was able ta nestle down next ta Billy an' fall into a deep sleep. Somewhere in that slumber, I found myself on the top of the ravine again. I was lookin' down into the knoll at a momma deer givin' birth. I couldn't quite make out what I was seein'. It appeared that instead of the slim little legs of a fawn emergin' from the momma, it was my pa's work boots bein' born. Then out of nowhere, Mel was standin' behind me. I spun 'round ta him, an' he knelt beside me.

"Birth. None of us 'member it. I hear it's a traumatic an' painful process. But it happens once ta every livin' creature that walks or crawls the face of God's green earth. Fer some of us, who give ourselves over ta God, we git born again in Him. It can also be a painful experience, but God gives us the strength ta see it through. You rest now, Pumpkin."

Mel kinda like disappeared an' I turned back ta the knoll. There stan'in' knee high in sweet grass was my pa. He was smilin' an' started walkin' towards me. His head was fine, an' his hair was clean an shiny. I felt so happy, so much at peace.

"Eula...Eula..." My name was bein' called an' I was bein' drawn out an' away from the woods, off the ridge of the ravine, an' worst, away from my Pa.

"Eula," called Aunt Lee. "Mornin', child. We're all takin' breakfast in the house. Come join us."

I rolled over on those hard wooden boards. The sun was comin' up over the tree line. Mel was stan'in' on Aunt Lee's back porch with a cup of coffee in hand. I got into the kitchen an' plopped down at the table. Everyone was a sleepy, kinda quiet.

"Have you talked ta my Momma?" I asked Aunt Lee.

"No, Honey. Uncle Joe an' her stayed in town last night with your pa."

"When are we goin inta town?" Billy asked.

"We're gonna stay here till we hear from 'em," Aunt Lee told Billy.

Mel looked out the side window then stepped out the back door. My ears caught the sound of a wagon comin' up ta the house. I was out of my seat lickety split, closely followed by little Bill. It was Uncle

Joe. He was alone. Somehow that seemed good ta me. Mel took the bridle of Uncle Joe's horse an' steadied 'im while Uncle Joe climbed down. He looked haggard, a man without sleep. I searched his face fer some kinda inklin' as ta my father's fate. As Aunt Lee joined us, he broke into a weak smile.

"He woke up this mornin', an' asked if his order had been filled at the mill. He didn't 'member a thin'. He said he has a powerful headache an' wants ta come home."

Billy jumped on me huggin' my neck an' kissin' my face. The girls screamed with joy as we all clung onto each other so we wouldn't float off into space. Aunt Lee hugged Uncle Joe's neck an' started cryin'. I went up

ta Mel an' put my arms 'round his waist, givin' him a family hug as well.

"Now hold on, here. Your Pa is still hurt bad, an' he won't be a comin' home just yet. He an' your momma have ta go on up ta Vicksburg ta the hospital there on accounta Doc Horne can't give him the treatment he needs. His skull has been fractured an' them doctors gotta check him over. He'll be off his feet quite a spell."

I later heard tell that Pa's brain was actually bare ta the world; this is why everyone thought he was dead. Aunt Lee went with us ta our house ta pack up some clothes fer Pa an' Momma, fer their trip ta

Vicksburg. Mel stayed with the girls at our house. Mel was gonna tend the hogs, an' the girls were gonna help with feedin' the stock an' chickens.

Chapter 16

The trip ta town ta see Pa was so different from yesterday. Today there was a breeze in my face, the sun was on my back, an' the birds were sin'in'. We were so anxious ta git there we could hardly contain ourselves. Uncle Joe told us ta settle down cause we was gettin' on Lucille's nerves. I don't think children's noise makes a horse nervous, but I'm sure it can bother a man who's had no sleep. As we got into town, we was waved at an' well wished by every one we saw. We felt like we was in a parade on the fourth of July. We got ta the Doc's office an' Momma come out the door; she had been watchin' fer us. We jumped from the wagon an' ran ta her. She hugged an' kissed our necks an' knelt down an' explained Pa was still hurt an' we couldn't be jumpin' up on his bed. We had ta be quiet as church mice when we went in. She also warned us he was all ban'aged up an' his face was swollen an' bruised where the keg of nails had fell from a shelf an' hit him.

She told us after we visited with him, they were gonna be driven ta Vicksburg by Mr. Parker in his truck. Mr. Parker was one of the richest men in the county, an' he offered 'em a ride there an' back. I 'member walkin' into the Doc's office. It had that clean an' sterile kinda smell. There was rooms fer patients if'n they need ta be watched over by the Doc. When we came in, the doctor asked Billy how his leg was, which was the furtherest thin' from Billy's mind. Doc instructed us on not ta get on the bed an' jostle Pa 'round.

"Hi, you two," Pa said. "I guess I gave you all a scare. I'm sorry 'bout all that."

He reached out his hand, which Billy an' I clung on ta. His face was swollen an' bruised, but I never saw him look prettier. His speech was slow, but his grip was firm an' gentle.

'We ask you ta restore him completely ta his family.' Mel's words come into my mind. I kissed my Pa's hand an' put my forehead ta it, thankin' God fer listenin' ta the hearts an' prayers of a child.

"Pa, do you 'member gittin' hit in the head?" Billy asked.

"I don't 'member anythin' 'til I felt someone a squeezin' my leg.

Then I kinda trembled all over. An' I 'member bein' cold, but then I started warmin' up. That's all I can 'member."

I could tell Pa was a bit frustrated at not bein' able ta recall his time. I couldn't help but wonder if'n Mel's touchin' Pa's leg had anythin' ta do with Pa bein' healed. I was sure God had sent Mel ta us.

"We all prayed fer ya Pa, an' God heard us. He heard our prayers an' gave you back ta us," I said believin' the credit belonged ta the Almighty.

"Thank you fer prayin' fer me, Honey. He did hear you," Pa said.

"Pa, you gotta ta go ta church with us from now on," I pleaded. "We gotta go as a family."

I felt we had ta pay God back somehow. We had ta show Him we was thankful. I didn't want God ta think we was an ungrateful lot. I didn't want God ta ever think he was mistaken by his goodness ta us.

"Honey, we will, soon as I can well all go ta Meetin'," Pa promised his baby girl.

"Mr. Parker's outside," Doc Horne informed us. "It time ta git you up ta Vicksburg."

With that, there were gentle kisses an' squeezes of good-byes an' last minutes instructions on behavin' fer Aunt Lee while they were away. We loaded up in the wagon as Pa was carried off ta the truck. Mr. Parker had parked it in front. Momma an' Pa was restin' in the back makin' ready fer the long ride in front of 'em. Pastor Blanchard blessed their trip an' asked God ta be with 'em an' ta help ease Pa's pain. An' they were off. We watched as the tires from the truck kicked up dust as they spun out of town. A great peace came over me, a peace I think Mel experienced when he fell through the ice up the Michigan way. I was no longer fearful.

Dread didn't pull at every hair on my body. I could rest in the peace that God was taken care of my Pa. We headed home in the back of that old wagon. Billy didn't say a word. He'd just smile at me from time ta time. As we was passin' over Thornapple Creek, Billy shouted, "Look Uncle Joe!" He stopped the wagon abruptly.

Down, off the road where the creek turned back into the woods stood that white fawn, his head held high, his ears pointin' ta the sky. He stood there, starin' at us intently, his white coat a twitchin' ta keep the gallinippers an' mosquitoes from a bitin' 'im.

"It's an omen," Billy said. "A sign Pa's gonna be okay. Mel said that the Indians believed it was a powerful sign - a sign of peace an' families comin' together..."

"An' he said it was a powerful religious sign. Maybe a change is comin' on." I wondered out loud. Maybe a change in Pa, I wondered in my heart.

In one bound, the "white promise" had vanished with little more than a twitch of a branch. We'd never see or hear of that animal again.

"Why that was the prettiest thin' I ever did see,"

Aunt Lee said.

"Never saw a white deer before. I bet they'd pay a pretty penny fer the hide down Baton Rouge way," Uncle Joe said.

I looked at Billy. Now I knew where he got in from.

"Them kinda animals aren't fer huntin', Uncle Joe, they're fer enjoyin' an' fer watchin' in wonder," Billy taught, a lesson well learned. We got back ta Uncle Joe's an' dropped off Aunt Lee. We went ta our house ta pick up the girls, an' ta let Mel know what all was goin' on. Mel had taken care of the hogs an' was finishin' the last panel on the barn sidin'.

"Mel," Uncle Joe started, "we're taken Eula an' Billy ta stay with us 'til Annie an' Otis git back. Annie asked if ya'd mind stayin' in the house 'til their return. You can use the back room. Make yourself ta home. Annie said you knew where the coffee an' food was, so just ta go on an' make fer yourself. You come down an' take meals with us," Uncle Joe invited.

"Well thank you,, Joe. I'll be here tendin' the pigs an' hogs; I'll be hoin' on the fields till Otis is able; don't you worry none."

We headed back ta Uncle Joe's with our sacks packed with clothes, an all we'd need ta stay fer a long visit. If we really needed anythin', we could run home an' git it. Uncle Joe set up the rules from the git go. No runnin' in the house, no jumpin' on beds, no goin' home without 'em knowin', an' a host of others. If'n you was doin' somethin' he didn't like, it got added ta the list. I heard Uncle Joe come in one mornin' fer breakfast an' tell how

he'd gone down ta git the pigs fed before daybreak. Mel was up an' almost done with the chore! He'd been a workin' ta lantern light, pumpin' the water reservoir full of water, feedin' 'em their slop. He collected the eggs from the chicken coop an' scraped it clean, too.

"He's a good man, the kind worth havin' as kin," Uncle Joe said.

It was a long nine days' fere Momma an' Pa got home. He was still ban'aged up, but the swellin' had gone down. His face was a bit yellowish from bruisin', but his smile was big an' broad. He hugged us long, an' he hugged us hard. Momma asked Mel ta stay on in the house so he could help with Pa if'n she needed it. Mr. Moyer came by with chunks of smoked an' fresh meats. He was brin'in' Pa beefsteaks everyday, "'cause your pa needs ta git his strength back," he would say.

I heard Mr. Moyer went an' paid off Pa's bill at Marie's an' told her ta let him take care of our bills 'til Pa was back on his feet. Turned out Mr. Moyer was a pretty wealthy man. He brought over the pack of pups one day, an' Billy picked himself out the runt of the litter, which grew into a horse weighin' out fifty pounds or better. Mel worked the farm hard the next few weeks. Zeb, a colored man who worked a piece of property down from Uncle Joe, came an' worked the fields a bit every day. Never did find out who paid him, but I always suspected it was Mr. Moyer. One evenin' Pa an' Mel were takin' coffee out on the front porch. I was sittin' in the front room next ta the open window, listenin' ta grown-up conversation.

"Mel, I'll always be in your debt fer all you've done 'round here. I want you ta know you'll always have a place ta hang your hat here," Pa said as he looked out over the front fields.

I was sittin' ta the side of Pa an' I could see the tears of a grateful heart wellin' up. Mel took a deep breath, lookin' over those same fields.

"Otis, you have a great life here, an' a wonderful family to share it all with.

God's seen fit to give you a second chance. Embrace it, Otis. You are the leader of this family. You're their protector, an' provider. Be their spiritual strength, too. I'm askin' you to turn your life completely over to Jesus Christ, Lord an' Savior. He delivered you from death's doorstep, back into the arms of your loved ones. An' none of that is worth a hill of beans without a relationship with Him. If'n I spoke out of turn, well, I care 'bout you all, an' I reckon that gives me the right."

Mel took a sip of his coffee. I never heard anyone speak so plainly ta Pa.

"You have the right. You're family as far as I'm concerned. Mel, I got ta know somethin'," Pa asked. "Who are you? An' what did you do ta me when I was layin' on that bench?"

Pa's head slowly turned, an' his eyes locked on Mel's. Mel looked away back over the fields an' sipped some more of his coffee, then placed it down on the table next ta his chair. He had a sense of authority 'bout him; it was his words Pa had ta deal with.

"Otis, I'm a child of God's same as you, blessed, loved an' fergiven. I'm just makin' my way through this world, spreadin' His truth here an' there, bein' an instrument of his grace an' demonstratin' his love to all who reach out, as well as to those who choose not to."

"Otis, I did nothin' to you while your life was drippin' away, as you laid there on that bench. I will say, the prayers of a child were heard. I believe you know you were touched an' given a second chance. Surrender your will an' your way. Follow the One who sought you out an' restored your life."

With that, Mel stood up an' placed his hand on Pa's shoulder.

"May God bless this home an' this family, today an' always. I'll be leavin' in the mornin' after breakfast. You'll be gettin' on better each day. Thin's 'round here are gonna be looked after by Zeb an' his two boys. They'll be comin' to help with the chores, fer the rest of the season. You tell 'em what you want done they'll take care of it. ,They've been paid, so you don't need to be worryin' on that. It's time fer me to be movin' on. You get a good night's sleep. I'll see ya in the mornin'." Mel walked down the stairs an' disappeared 'round the side of the house. I couldn't believe it! Mel was leavin', an' now I knew Pa thought he was special, too. I went outside an' looked 'round fer Mel. I couldn't find him. It was gettin'' on toward bedtime an' Momma was tuckin' us in. "Mel's leavin tomorrow," I told Momma.

"Yes, I know, child, Pa told me."

"I can't believe he's goin'!" I said. "Pa still needs his help."

"We'll be fine. Pa's gittin' stronger everyday, an' help's been arranged," Momma assured.

"Where's he goin? Will he be back?" I asked.

"Honey, he's headed west, out ta California, just like he was when he stopped off here an' helped out 'round here. Now go ta sleep an' git some rest."

'Mel was leavin',' I thought. It seemed like just this mornin' he walked right passed me an' picked Little Bill up outta the creek. My little heart knew he was sent ta us by God. I hadn't understood some of the thin's I had seen, but the plain truth was, we was better off havin' him with us fer a spell. There would be a powerful hole ta fill with Mel bein' gone. But somehow I knew someone else was out there who needed ta know him an' the One he served. An' knowin' that was the only thin' that could make sense in sayin' good-bye. I had a pain in my heart that shot down ta my toes think'n 'bout Mel not be here. A pain that is reserved fer those you love. I would always love that man with the shinny clothes an' a satchel 'round his neck, an' my prayers would be with him each day.

I awoke the next mornin' ta the smell of bacon an' ham bein' fried up. I hurried down stairs, not wantin' ta miss a moment with Mel. Halfway I stopped an' ran back ta my room. I went ta my dresser an' removed my cross pendant from its home. I placed it 'round my neck an' flew down the stairs. There I found the whole family sittin' an' sippin' coffee. Mel was wearin' the shirt Momma had made fer him. Momma was makin' flapjacks, eggs, bacon an' ham. One pan had fried potatoes. This was a big send-off breakfast. When I sat down, there was a collection of animals 'round my plate. Mel had carved a raccoon, a bear, a sheep an' a tiger, one of each fer Billy an' me.

"Mel, these are so nice. Thank you so very much," I said.

"You're welcome, Pumpkin. I hope you an' Billy will say a prayer fer me every now an' then when your playin' with 'em."

Our breakfast was filled with stories of grabbin' catfish, playin' horseshoes, catchin' gators, an' waterin' inventions of one kind an' another. Mel laughed at himself when Pa' membered Mel's story of stan'in' in the river gettin' his photograph took. Momma started cleanin' up an' packed a little somethin fer Mel ta take on the road.

"I have one more thin' fer you two before I go. It's out back on the table."

Billy an' I ran out the back door. Ta our amazement, we found a giant boat, an ark, on the table. It was a work of art. It was beautiful. It stood twenty-four inches high. You could open it like a storybook. It had three floors inside ta keep all the animals Mel had carved. There were Bible scriptures engraved all over it, as well as other animals carved into the wood.

"Well, you know what I'm talkin' 'bout. I gave it ta you as a child," the old woman said to her "boy". "I've watched you an' your children play with it."

"Yes, you have, Grammy," he conceded.

"What happened to Mel?" her boy asked.

"Don't rightly know. We never heard from him again. I 'member watchin' him walk down the road 'til he was clean out of sight."

The boy gave his grandmother a drink of the melted ice.

"Mel was a fascinatin' soul. I believe he changed my Pa's life. After Mel left, Pa got stronger, an' we all went ta church together, every Sunday. Pa walked forward one Sunday mornin', ta our surprise, at the end of a service. No alter call had been given, it was just his time, he said, no reason ta wait, God had been waitin' on him long enough. Standin' in front of the whole congregation, he surrendered his life ta his Lord an' Savior publicly. Pa was asked ta be a deacon where he served over thirty-five years. Billy grew up an' became a preacher ta that little church we attended. He traces the start of his spiritual journey ta that ark an' those carved pieces of wood Mel made fer us.

"Boy, it's time you be needin' ta git on home," the old woman noticed.

"Oh, I'm fine, Grammy," the "boy" protested.

"Well, I'm sleepy, an' I'll rest better knowin' you're on your way home."

He bent over and kissed her on the forehead and gently brushed her hair from her eyes.

"Good night, Pumpkin." He smiled. "You sleep good," he requested of her fondly.

"You, too, my sweet boy. You, too. Thank you fer listenin' ta the ramblin's of an old woman."

Before leaving the room, he looked back from the

doorway; lying beneath those covers was a great blessing. She was a child of God's, she had been deeply blessed, loved, and forgiven by Him. With his eyes fixed on her small form, he prayed before he left...

"Lord, this woman has been an instrument of your grace and a demonstration of your love. She has been an example throughout my life, thank-you. I pray she'll find rest in you tonight, and I praise your name for having been able to see glimpses of you through her eyes. Amen.

Melchizedek...
Without father or mother, without genealogy,
Without beginning of days, or end of life...
like the Son of God, he remains a priest forever.
Hebrews 7:3

MEL
1928

Mel is sighted a number of years later. This time in the cities and
   jungles of Siam, which is now known as Thailand. The year is 1928; in his
   walk, he crosses paths with the life of a young

gemstone hunter. Alan Caplan's gods are wealth and rocks he finds in the earth. Mel will show this man the most precious gem the earth has ever held. As well as a path he would have never considered walking down.

About the Author

Danny Sarros was born and raised in Chicago and the city's western suburbs. He holds a Graduate Gemologist degree from the Gemological Institute of America, and continues to work as an international gem merchant. Danny is a natural born story teller with a fondness for detail that he uses to paint a more complete picture for his readers. He enjoys spending time with family and friends as well as the out doors. When not home, Danny can be found fishing in some remote spot in Canada or sitting around a campfire, telling stories while frying up the days catch.